Keto Living Cookbook
2

**Lose Weight with 101 Yummy & Low Carb Ketogenic
Savory and Sweet Snacks**

TABLE OF CONTENTS

SAVORY TEMPTATIONS

SWEET TEMPTATIONS

FOREWORD

My name is Ella, author of the first Keto Living Cookbook, and self-confessed lover all things food, and yes... this includes snacks!

All my life I have loved cooking and it's safe to say the miracle that is the Ketogenic diet literally turned my life around, helped me attain my ideal weight and with the right recipe, actually lets me have my cake *and* eat it too. ☺

Since writing the first book, I have received amazing support and encouragement from the Keto community.

Suggestions to make a full color cookbook with photos have been taken seriously and I have been in touch with my publisher and a leading food photographer in relation to making this dream a reality.

Others that are living Keto and are more focused on muscle building than fat loss have reminded me how useful the recipes translate to both goals, and not just losing weight.

However, the most popular request I've encountered was to put out a recipe book containing only a selection of my favorite snacks, on-the-go foods, and treats.

Some of you may be thinking, "Snacking on Keto? That can't be!"

The common myth when diving into a Ketogenic lifestyle is that once we remove the pasta, the bread, potatoes, and carbs in general, that we lose a lot of the fun foods and flavor along the way, especially when dieting.

This of course doesn't have to be the case.

101 Yummy and Low Carb Ketogenic Savory and Sweet Snacks

Let's admit it, almost all of us periodically suffer from the dreaded snack attack and I'm the first to agree with you that this is ok. Life is meant for living and I for one, am not ashamed of feeling like a tasty treat when the mood takes me.

We're only human after all! We deserve to be happy, and armed with the right recipes there's no need to accept a nibble free future!

So... how *do* we enjoy snacking and stay on track? What do we do when the cravings hit?

Staying in ketosis is key. The pre-packaged and processed chips, pretzels, candy and other temptations need to stay right where they are, on the shelves and in the shops.

Instead, with a bit of creative energy, careful ingredient selection, and the right recipes in the hands of a Keto connoisseur such as yourself, we can make mouth-watering masterpieces that are a delight to the palate and perfect for our lifestyle of living healthy, losing weight or body sculpting.

The goal is to be able to make portable and delicious Keto goodies that satisfy a hunger yet leave you feeling curiously guilt free in the blissful aftermath.

So this brings us to the other overwhelmingly positive comment received for the first Keto Living Cookbook, regarding the nutritional information calculated on every recipe.

There are many tools available to us. Ketostix, breath acetone detectors, blood Ketone meters and the list goes on in our journey to quantify ourselves and stay in a state of Ketosis.

My intention with this range of books is to provide another supportive tool in your arsenal to assist with keeping you on track, and reaching your goals whatever they may be, with nutritional info and net carbohydrate count per serving included for every single recipe.

This information has proved invaluable for many readers in helping choose suitable recipes, meals and portion sizes that fit within their personal macro allowance for each day.

So without further ado, ahead lies a cornucopia of nutritionally calculated, fantastic snacking pleasure.

Pizza, pancakes, muffins, and meatballs. Ice-cream, fat bombs, nutty delights, cakes, guacamole, burgers and more awaits.

The Keto Living Cookbook 2 contains 101 of my very favorite Ketogenic snack recipes, with easy-to-follow instructions and plenty of variety designed to leave you sighing with pleasure and coming back again and again.

There's rarely a need for any fancy equipment or for a vast range of ingredients. In fact, if you already follow a Keto lifestyle you will likely have a stock of many of the items required, already on the shelf.

I just know you're going to enjoy this collection of recipes in the Keto Living Cookbook 2 and I'm so happy to be able to be a part of your adventure towards a healthier new you!

Love and Keto for life!

Ella

DISCLAIMER

Before we get started, a quick note on the nutritional information found at the bottom of each recipe.

Simply put, I've done my best to fastidiously calculate the macro nutrient breakdown, however obviously there will be variations in everyone's exact kitchen creation, due mainly to brand choices, different cuts of meats, absorption of fats in frying etc.

So please, understand that as a general rule the numerical values should be fairly close in the calculations, and are included primarily to serve as a beneficial guide to keeping you on track in achieving your goals.

And as an FYI, the net carb count has been calculated by deducting the dietary fiber from the total carbohydrates.

I certainly hope that the info proves useful and accurate to you, and of course if you wish to double check my calculations on any recipe, I would always recommend that you please do so if you feel the need.

GRANULATED AND POWDERED SUGAR SUBSTITUTES

After much thought, I decided that in a book that includes some recipes that call for a granulated or powdered sugar substitute to be added as an ingredient in some cases, this information really needed to be shared to clear up a lot of the misinformation surrounding sugar alternatives available to us as consumers.

In cases where a recipe calls for a sugar substitute, we are of course looking to use a product that is for all intents and purposes a cup for cup exchange for sugar by volume, and one should attempt to use powdered for the recipes that require it, and granulated in those instances.

If you are choosing to purchase a store bought blend and can only find granulated, you can use a blender to make powdered if the recipe calls for it.

For our purposes where a sugar substitute is used in a recipe, in all nutritional panels this has been calculated and added to the totals as if the increasingly popular sweet polyol (or sugar alcohol), Erythritol was used, and this has been calculated at 0.2 carb calories per gram.

If however, you decide to use an alternative sweetener or create your own blend such as the **'Ella's All Purpose Mix'** example recipe provided at the end of this section, you would need to do a different nutritional calculation for each recipe accordingly.

Now, I think it's important to look at this more carefully, to understand the options available.

Every sugar substitute brand on the shelf contains different ingredients, the two main components being the sweetener itself, and if required a bulking agent to bring the product up to a cup for cup mix.

What we are of course looking for is the perfect balance of mouthfeel, texture, lowest carb content, and similarity in baking properties, and of course carries a history of product safety, and minimal if any discomfort from use.

If you don't want to overthink things at all, and just get straight to the kitchen, then your most basic baking sweetener alternative that requires the least amount of work and effort is to use pure Erythritol, a sugar alcohol.

Erythritol, when used in direct replacement for sugar is 70% as sweet as sugar with 90% absorbed in the small intestine and not metabolised, excreted unchanged in the urine and the remaining 10% only partially metabolised. These unique properties gives Erythritol a documented figure of only 0.2 calories per gram, as opposed to white table sugars 3.8 calories per gram.

Some loosely argue the calorie content is really even closer to zero, and that none is absorbed, and in fact is listed as such on labels in Japan and the United States. Others maintain that around 5-10% is absorbed, giving it a caloric count of approximately 0.24 calories per gram, which seems closer to scientific fact in my opinion.

Either way, this is a very nice low carb, low GI ingredient to use that is also dental friendly. There are minimal complaints of stomach upset, with reports of any kind of nausea only arising in sensitive individuals consuming over 50g of product per day, which in baking, is usually a fair amount of servings.

So for starting out, this is a good all round sugar substitute. If the 70% sweetness doesn't quite meet the grade, either a couple more tablespoons per cup can make it up without altering the structure of most recipes with any real detriment, or preferably I'd suggest adding a couple of drops of a liquid sweetener of your choice such as Stevia will also suffice, and add a nice synergy to the flavor.

Aside from Erythritol, almost all other Keto recommended sugar alternatives are so powerful in sweetness that many brands on the shelf need to use both a proprietary blend of a sweetener and some filler to make up the volume to a cup to cup approximation to sugar, more suited to baking.

With these blends, there are considerations with each and every combination.

So it's time to get educated on label reading.

First I should mention that when reading the nutritional information on the label of many cup to cup sugar substitute packages to exercise caution, as many products are outright listed as zero calories.

There appears to be a legislative loophole in some countries that classifies amounts as small as a teaspoon as a 'serving' and therefore negligible enough in calories to pass labelling guidelines as a zero calorie per serving product.

Obviously this leaves us without the full picture when using these products in larger quantities, a picture very important for our needs.

Although I could refer you straight to the manufacturer's web sites, and ingredient listings – even many of these websites are opting not to include this information, instead simply running with the 'Zero calorie' claims.

So it becomes up to us to do our research on what constitutes a sweetener, a sugar alcohol, and a filler and the potential uses of each. The most common with a few of my notes are as follows.

SWEETENERS

Agave Nectar (GI – 15)

I personally avoid this high carb option. It's less glycemic than glucose but has almost the same caloric result.

Aspartame (GI - 0)

With controversial results stemming from a lot of studies on excessive consumption of this sweetener, I wouldn't with any confidence, recommend Aspartame as a first choice. Also, at high temperatures, this artificial sweetener becomes unstable for baking, so for me, aspartame remains a no.

Monk fruit (Luo Han Guo) (GI - 0)

This sweetener is extracted from fruit and is 150x sweeter than sugar and is tasty as a carefully measured additive in a blend. Some brands makes an interesting mix of this and Erythritol to try and closely match the taste and 'cup for cup' usage of sugar.

Saccharine (GI - 0)

Not good for baking, and has a bitter aftertaste.

Stevia (GI - 0)

This glycoside extracted from the leaf of a plant, is 300x the sweetness of regular sugar, and also a popular choice. Over the years stevia has taken a bit of criticism, firstly for its well documented aftertaste reminiscent of liquorice, which seems to have been all but eliminated in the refined liquid form available from many brands.

Secondly, the jury seems to still not be completely finished with the safety of stevia. Reports and tests show that normal quantities are fine, but there were some unfortunate rats tested along the way in much larger dosages that didn't fare so well.

My verdict on Stevia personally, is that the small quantity required is suitable in general as an additive to a blend.

Sucralose (GI - 0)

At 600x strength and a flavor profile that very nearly matches sugar, this artificial sweetener needs to be added with a precise calculation, although again I should note that data is still being collected on the product and is no longer globally accepted as completely safe based on some studies of long term use.

POLYOLS OR SUGAR ALCOHOLS

In a category of their own, but also what we will list here as a sweetener are Sugar Alcohols, a class of polyol, but have no fear if you are sober, there contain no ethanol so it's not really that kind of alcohol!

Sugar alcohols occur naturally, and are often obtained through hydrogenation and fermentation processes.

Polyols used as a sugar substitute by most individuals will be fine, although each can cause varying degrees of gastro-intestinal complaints in high consumption in sensitive individuals.

Also the strength of sweetness and therefore volume in baking usage of a sugar alcohol is closer to that of sugar, in comparison to the many 100x or more strength options in the previous category.

All of these are low GI though, and the teeth don't seem to suffer as a rule either.

Erythritol (GI - 1)

Recommended - as mentioned above Erythritol is a no (to very low) GI polyol, contains only 0.2 calories / gram, is 70% as sweet as sugar when used cup for cup in place of sugar, and doesn't promote tooth decay.

Also, being absorbed in the small intestine gives it less of a laxative effect than other sugar alcohols.

Look for pure Erythritol with no fillers if seeking the lowest calorie product. Proprietary blends or careful adding of small amounts of other high strength sweeteners such as Stevia, Sucralose or Monk Fruit can work well in conjunction, and will not add significantly to caloric or carb content.

Maths is important here when working out quantities as some sweeteners are 100's of times stronger than regular sugar!

Also, larger doses over 50g in a day has been known to potentially bring about side effects in particularly sensitive individuals such as hives, stomach rumbling and nausea. Also increased urination and thirst is pretty common with all sugar alcohols.

Anecdotally, it appears that Erythritol can also have a drying effect on some foods – so it's fine in moister recipes, but use your judgement, and perhaps compensate with a dryer baked recipe by adding a little xanthum gum and cream cheese for example.

In the same vein, a no bake cheese cake for example with no liquid ingredient may suffer using Erythritol with drying / recrystallizing.

Lastly, not all but some report an unusual taste in certain final products, such as when chocolate, coffee or peanut butter is the main component of the dish.

Glycerol / Glycerine (GI - 5)

In most cases, I would suggest to avoid – Glycerine has about 2/3 the sweetening power as regular sugar and it actually contains **slightly more calories** than sugar, having 27 calories per teaspoon versus sugar's 20 calories. However, a teaspoon or two of this can be used in ice-cream as a powerful freezing point depressor, and to help reduce ice crystals from forming. Also the taste will suffer above this quantity and on a Keto diet I'm careful not to add too much, or instead use an alternative.

Sorbitol (GI - 4)

Avoid overall, it has about 3/4 the sweetening power as regular sugar, with about 2/3 the calories, also carries a slight effect on blood sugar, and a pronounced laxative effect.

Xylitol (GI - 12)

For Keto specifically, I mainly steer clear of this sugar substitute. In general however, it has some positives.

It's cup for cup in usage, and just as sweet as sugar, actually has properties beneficial to dental health, and the GI is only 12, but... it contains just 40% less calories than sugar, so in general depending on the recipe requirement, this is too high if we want to reduce carbs, which we do – that being said, Xylitol could possibly be used minimally in a blend if the taste appealed and the mix benefitted the recipe. As with many sugar alcohols though, Xylitol can have a laxative effect.

Please be aware, although most other polyols are safe if ingested by a pet, **Xylitol is toxic to dogs, cats and other pets**, so if you use this polyol, don't leave your leftovers near your canine companion!

Isomalt (GI - 2), **Lactitol** (GI - 3), **Mannitol** (GI - 2)

all have about half the sweetening power as regular sugar, with half the calories give or take, and based on this I would avoid these.

Maltitol (GI - 35)

I avoid anything containing Maltitol, as it is still heavy in calories and has a pronounced effect on blood sugar. If you read the side of many 'Low-Carb' protein bars, look for the Maltitol content. In my opinion, you should tread carefully to avoid a potential trap.

FILLERS

Whether you'll find a filler or not in a product on the shelf, or if you need to include one in a blend you mix up yourself at home depends on a couple of factors.

Firstly, the maths behind the sweetness intensity per volume of sugar substitute needs to be calculated, and secondly, a scientific benefit inherent from the addition of certain fillers is often a recipe dependent factor, which we will get into in a moment.

Below are a few of the more commonly known fillers, and some notes on each.

Maltodextrin (GI - 110) and **Dextrose** (GI - 100)

Avoid as these bulking agents contain a very high GI and a near carb/calorie per gram count as sugar (**Sucrose** *has a Glycemic Index of 100*).

Polydextrose (GI - 6)

OK – now this is a synthetic polymer synthesized from dextrose and a pretty good filler in moderation, it has an overall good profile, sporting a low GI and a caloric value of around 1 calorie per gram.

This can certainly add up quickly, although once you know your substitutes well, using Polydextrose in some recipes can give better results as an alternative or blended into certain creations.

For instance, it's a pretty good freezing point depressor similar in some ways to sugar. Ice-cream benefits in overall 'scoopability' by including Polydextrose in a sugar substitute blend.

Polydextrose actually also has some sweetness, but by itself will not usually be sweet enough, and as with fillers in general, will require a sweetener added.

As an aside, for a non-baked application, dissolving the Polydextrose first in a warm liquid is fairly essential.

Some people do report digestive issues consuming Polydextrose, and therefore quantity should be measured with care.

Also, having recently gone a little out of style a little in low carb circles, it's a reasonably difficult ingredient to track down and may require some research to find if attempting to use this in a blend.

Inulin and Oligofructose (GI - 1)

These are also a good option in a blend, with similar properties to Polydextrose.

Often extracted from chicory root or synthesized from sucrose, these fiber fillers contain around 1.5 calories per gram, anecdotally this can be less in some individuals depending on how each person processes fiber of this nature.

Benefits in a blend that includes Erythritol, may include hiding the cooling effect Erythritol carries.

Again, these fibers can cause gastro-intestinal issues in above average doses.

A WORD ON BLENDS AND BRANDS

The combinations you can find on the shelves, many touting 'Zero calorie' claims is quite extensive.

Maltodextrin and Sucralose could be the contents of one blend, or you may discover a higher priced but nicely reviewed Erythritol and Monk Fruit. Some blends are found containing Oligofructose, or Inulin / Chicory Root is popular, then there is some that contain Polydextrose, and some may use a percentage of a combination of sweeteners but still also use a percentage white sugar as an ingredient in an attempt to advertise loudly their 'tastes like sugar, reduced calorie brand'.

And with blend in hand, some experimenting bakers may also add additional bulk to a recipe with scientifically measured portions of Guar or Xanthan Gum, Psyllium Husk, or other fibers or ingredients for additional structure and integrity.

ELLA'S ALL PURPOSE MIX

In making our own sugar substitute, the ultimate goal for us in a blend is to mimic sweetness, and add bulk while heavily reducing carbs and calories, and of course GI keeping in mind that sweeteners often combine synergistically in a way that makes a more natural product.

For a pretty good all round very low GI baking 'sugar', I often use 75% pure Erythritol, 25% Polydextrose or Inulin, and a carefully measured amount of luo han guo, sucralose, or stevia to taste.

In addition, ultimately the best mix will vary depending on exactly what you are trying to cook.

THE ICE-CREAM EXAMPLE

Sometimes we need to revisit our blend to better suit a recipe. For example, the hardness of ice-cream is largely controlled by the combination of sweeteners used, as there are various freezing points for each.

Without getting too technical, regular sucrose has a freezing point of 1.0x, Erythritol is 2.8x this, and Polydextrose is 0.6x – so it may be advisable to add more Polydextrose and less Erythritol to get the consistency just right when building a sugar substitute for this icy treat.

Maltodextrin, aside from its other reasons as a poor choice has a freezing point of 0.1x, so unless you want a brick of ice-cream in the fridge, you'd avoid anything containing this.

In fact, with ice cream there are many tricks to get the consistency just right. As your experimentation deepens, you may find yourself adding a teaspoon or two of glycerine (see notes for why in **Glycerine** above).

Or, you may even opt to add a couple of tablespoons of vodka to a liter. This will have a similar benefit, but will effectively churn up an 'adults only batch'. The alcohol doesn't freeze so the end product is again, more scoopable – but of course, if making this batch, you should be careful the kids don't get into it!

And to continue to add to the ice-cream confusion, too much Polydextrose can be too gummy, and too much Erythritol can cause crystallization.

Oh, the joys of cooking! Ice-cream in particular however, is a delicate flower to work with, that's for certain.

IN CONCLUSION

So in conclusion, the *simplest* and lowest carb choice is to bake with the sugar alcohol Erythritol, keeping aware of how your body reacts to amounts around or over 50g a day, and being careful to watch how certain recipes handle the ingredient, and your overall enjoyment of the taste and level of sweetness.

As you enter the slightly more complex experimentation phase, adding different sweeteners will create some lovely synergy and is in some cases mandatory for a really effective flavor, and adjusting the balance of Erythritol to include a varying ratio of Polydextrose or Inulin will give different results again, depending on the science and structure of the dish taking into account a variety of factors such as dish dryness, flavor, freezing point requirements etc.

Almost everyone will find or create a mix or a brand that works perfectly for them with just a little research, and when you do, you'll have even greater confidence in cooking these dishes.

In the meantime, please experiment yourself, or try my **'Ella's All Purpose Mix'**. Most importantly have fun with the recipes ahead, only a handful of them use a sugar substitute, but this is good information to carry with you from hereon.

LIQUID SUGAR SUBSTITUTES

As several of the sweet recipes call for a liquid sweetener sugar substitute instead of a powdered or granular option, it's important to add this note to the book on quantities used.

We discussed sweeteners such as Stevia, and Sucralose in the last section, and these are often available in liquid drops.

For our purposes, I have kept things reasonably simple, and wherever there is an ingredient listing for a liquid sugar substitute, I have simply used liquid Stevia.

However, to complicate things just a little, different brands of Stevia extract can have a varying strength sweetness depending on the actual percentage of Steviol content added to the product.

Also brand dependant, there is variety in taste and bitterness of Stevia depending on whether the Steviol extracted from the plant are either Steviosides or Rebaudiosides (less bitter, and almost 50% sweeter), and this isn't always marked clearly on the label.

I personally prefer the flavor of a stevia sweetener made with as close to 100% Rebaudiosides as possible, however individual tastes may vary.

So in closing, wherever you see liquid sweetener used in a recipe, this is what I have used as my ingredient, and measurements have been calculated accordingly, which works out to about a teaspoon of product being the equivalent of a cup of sugar.

Depending on brand, or if using an alternative such as Sucralose which is doubly strong in sweetness, you will need to adjust quantities accordingly, and the taste test is usually best practice!

SAVORY
TEMPTATIONS

SKEWERED LAMB FILLET WITH ROSEMARY

A canapé for a special occasion or just for your pure indulgence!

Makes 20

INGREDIENTS:

1 tbsp. ground cumin

1 tbsp. ground turmeric

3 drops liquid stevia extract (adjust to taste)

1 tbsp. hazelnut oil (or other nut oil)

2 cloves garlic, crushed

1 tbsp. fresh cilantro, chopped

2 star anise, ground

Salt and pepper to season

2 pounds (908g) lamb fillet

1 small bunch fresh mint, chopped

4 ounces (113g) thick plain yogurt

Vegetable oil for frying

20 rosemary stalks

DIRECTIONS:

1. Mix together the first seven ingredients in a large ceramic bowl.

2. Season to taste.

3. Cut the lamb into strips and place in the same bowl.

4. Marinade for at least 3 hours or overnight.

5. Mix together the chopped mint and yogurt.

6. When you are ready to cook, thread the lamb onto the rosemary skewers and fry them over a high heat in a little

vegetable oil until nicely browned.

7. Serve with the yogurt and mint dip in a bowl.

Nutritional Facts per skewer: Calories 108, Fat 5.1g, Carbohydrate 0.8g, Dietary Fiber 0g, Net Carbs 0.8g, Protein 13.5g.

CUCUMBER AND AVOCADO CROÛTES

A crunchy snack which is easy to prepare and looks amazing with fres. green colors. Experiment using tuna instead. Also good with some finely chopped, hard-boiled egg on top!

Makes 20

INGREDIENTS:

1 cucumber, cut into 20 x ¼ inch (0.6cm) slices

8 ounces (227g) cream cheese

1 large, ripe avocado

Lemon juice to taste

A few drops Tabasco sauce (chili sauce)

Green onion slices

4 ounce (113g) can red salmon, flaked

DIRECTIONS:

1. Remove the avocado flesh from the skin and discard the pip.

2. Mash the avocado together with the cream cheese and beat well until smooth.

3. Season to taste with a little lemon juice and a few drops Tabasco.

4. Spoon, or pipe the mixture evenly onto the cucumber slices.

5. Top with some flaked salmon and a twist of sliced spring onion.

6. Serve.

Nutritional Facts per croûte: Calories 72, Fat 6.3g, Carbohydrate 2.3g, Dietary Fiber 1.0g, Net Carbs 1.3g, Protein 2.4g

Sweet Snacks

...AFERS

...rve, as they are or with a soft dip. These
...ainer. Try using different nuts in the recipe or
...you like.

INGREDIENTS:

1 tbsp. butter, unsalted

6 ounces (170g) parmesan cheese, finely shredded

2 tbsp. walnuts, finely chopped

Fresh thyme

DIRECTIONS:

1. Pre-heat the oven to 350°F (177°C).

2. Line several baking trays with parchment or grease proof paper.

3. Combine the butter and cheese together in a food processor or by hand.

4. Mix in the walnuts.

5. Drop spoonfuls, well apart, on the prepared trays.

6. Sprinkle with some fresh thyme.

7. Brown in the oven for about 8 minutes.

8. Remove from the oven and leave on the tray for a minute to set.

9. Remove the crisps and cool completely on a wire rack.

Nutritional Facts per wafer: Calories 19, Fat 1.4g, Carbohydrate 0.3g, Dietary Fiber 0g, Net Carbs 0.3g, Protein 1.5g

MOZZARELLA BATONS

Pop in your mouth finger food for entertaining or an everyday treat!

Serves 8

INGREDIENTS:

3 lemons

1 pound (454g) fresh mozzarella cheese

2 large garlic cloves, crushed

½ tsp. salt

½ cup (119ml) olive oil

Fresh thyme, finely chopped

DIRECTIONS:

1. Heat a griddle pan over a medium heat

2. Cut 12 thin slices from the lemons and squeeze the rest to give approximately 4 tablespoons of juice.

3. Cut the cheese into long rectangles, each about ¼ inch (0.6cm) thick.

4. In a small bowl mix together the crushed garlic and the salt.

5. Using a small spoon add the lemon juice and mix to a paste.

6. Whisk in enough of the olive oil to make a mayonnaise type consistency.

7. Toss the lemon slices and the cheese batons in this mixture.

8. Place on the griddle pan and griddle for 2 – 3 minutes, turning half way through.

9. Remove from the heat, place on a serving platter and sprinkle with thyme before serving.

Nutritional Facts per serving: Calories 286, Fat 24.1g, Carbohydrate 4.8g, Dietary Fiber 0.9g, Net Carbs 3.9g, Protein 15.1g.

ORIENTAL BEEF BALLS

Tiny beefy meatballs to serve as they are or on cocktail sticks with a dipping sauce – soy-ginger tastes good and adds a great tang!

Makes 30

INGREDIENTS:

1 pound (454g) ground beef

1 ounce (28g) onion, very finely chopped

1 fresh egg

½ tsp. salt

Pinch black pepper

2 cloves garlic, minced

FOR THE SAUCE:

¼ cup (59ml) soy sauce

2 tbsp. rice wine vinegar

1 tbsp. fresh ginger, grated

1 tbsp. green onion, chopped

1 clove garlic, minced

2 drops liquid stevia extract (adjust to taste)

DIRECTIONS:

1. Pre-heat the oven to 425°F (218°C).

2. Have ready a baking sheet with a rim.

3. Put all of the ingredients for the beef balls into a bowl and mix together lightly with your hands.

4. Shape the meat into small balls about 1 inch (2.5cm) in diameter.

5. Place on the baking tray and bake in the oven for about 12 minutes until brown but not dry. Make sure that they are cooked through!

6. Next, place all of the sauce ingredients in a small bowl and mix well together.

7. Place each meat ball on a cocktail stick and serve on a plate around the dipping sauce.

Nutritional Facts per meat ball: Calories 34, Fat 1.1g, Carbohydrate 0.5g, Dietary Fiber 0g, Net Carbs 0.5g, Protein 4.9g

CHEESY SAUSAGE BALLS

A hearty breakfast dish that is delicious, filling and extra cheesy!

Makes 24

INGREDIENTS:

24 ounces (680g) pork breakfast sausage

12 ounces (340g) Cheddar cheese, shredded

24 small cubes Cheddar cheese

Fat for frying

DIRECTIONS:

1. Remove the sausage meat from the skins and place in a large bowl.

2. Mix in the shredded cheese and blend well.

3. Form into 24 balls of equal size with your hands- mold the sausage around the cubes of Cheddar – lightly dampen your hands with water if the mixture sticks.

4. Heat the fat in a deep skillet and fry the sausage balls until brown on all sides and crisp.

5. Serve warm.

Nutritional Facts per portion: Calories 189, Fat 16.9g, Carbohydrate 0.4g, Dietary Fiber 0g, Net Carbs 0.4g, Protein 8.9g.

OVEN BAKED PARMESAN CHICKEN BITES

Well, chicken balls if you prefer, dressed in sauce and topped with cheese! This dish can be made in individual oven proof dishes and will re-heat well if kept in the fridge

Makes 24

INGREDIENTS:

1 pound (454g) white chicken breast meat, ground

1 cup (96g) almond flour

½ cup (50g) parmesan cheese, shredded

½ cup (237ml) unsweetened almond milk

1 tsp. salt

Pinch black pepper

½ tsp. dried oregano

1 cup (237ml) marinara sauce

3 ounces (85g) fresh mozzarella cheese

DIRECTIONS:

1. Pre-heat the oven to 350°F (177°C).

2. Grease an ovenproof dish and set aside.

3. In a large bowl mix together half of the almond flour, the parmesan, milk, seasonings and herbs.

4. Add the chicken and stir until just combined.

5. Divide the mixture into 24 portions and gently roll each into a ball.

6. Roll each ball in the remaining almond flour to coat and place in the greased ovenproof dish.

7. Place the dish in the oven and bake for 20 minutes turning once.

8. When done spoon the marinara sauce over the balls and top each with a small slice of mozzarella cheese.

9. Bake for a further 15 minutes until piping hot and the cheese is beginning to melt.

10. Remove from the oven and sprinkle with dried oregano.

Nutritional Facts chicken ball: Calories 72, Fat 3.1, Carbohydrate 2.2g, Dietary Fiber 0g, Net Carbs 2.2g, Protein 8.6g.

SALAMI ROLL UPS

Delicious Salami slices rolled up around a creamy cheese filling – a great lunch time treat. Cut smaller, or use smaller diameter salami for a Keto party snack option!

Makes 8

INGREDIENTS:

8 large slices salami

8 ounces (227g) cream cheese

½ cup (119ml) plain yogurt

3 cloves garlic, finely chopped

Dash Worcestershire sauce

Salt and pepper to taste

DIRECTIONS:

1. Mix together all of the ingredients except the salami.

2. Divide into eight even portions.

3. Place one portion along the middle of a slice of salami.

4. Roll up from one side.

5. Repeat with the rest of the mixture.

Nutritional Facts per roll: Calories 170, Fat 14.6g, Carbohydrate 3.1g, Dietary Fiber 0g, Net Carbs 3.1g, Protein 6.7g.

STUFFED PEPPER POPPERS

Sweet baby peppers with an avocado and bacon filling – delicious pop in the mouth snack for any time of the day. Easy to make too!

Makes 12

INGREDIENTS:

12 baby bell peppers, red or yellow

2 large ripe avocados

1 small lemon, juiced

¼ cup (4g) cilantro, chopped

1 tsp. hot chili sauce

12 rashers bacon

Salt and pepper to taste

DIRECTIONS:

1. Pre-heat the oven to 375°F (191°C).

2. Cut the peppers lengthwise into halves and remove the seeds and any membrane

3. Place on a baking sheet and bake for about 12 minutes until tender but not so soft that they collapse! Remove from the oven.

4. Meanwhile, fry the bacon in a large skillet until brown and crisp. Drain on paper towel to cool.

5. Crumble the bacon or chop very finely.

6. Prepare the filling by mashing together the avocado flesh, with the lemon juice, cilantro, chili sauce and seasoning to taste.

7. Mix in the crumbled bacon.

8. Using a teaspoon fill the peppers with the avocado mixture and enjoy.

9. These poppers don't keep well so eat them up and make some more!

Nutritional Facts per popper: Calories 141, Fat 10.8g, Carbohydrate 4.6g, Dietary Fiber 2.6g, Net Carbs 2.0g, Protein 8.8g.

AVOCADO GUACAMOLE

A traditional, all-time favorite! Enjoy every which way you desire!

1 large bowl serves 12

INGREDIENTS:

3 ripe avocados

2 tablespoons of freshly squeezed lime juice

1 small shallot or red onion very finely chopped

Salt and freshly ground pepper to taste

Paprika or a little cayenne pepper to garnish

DIRECTIONS:

1. Cut the avocados in half lengthwise and remove the pit.

2. Peel the skin off and dice half of the flesh into a large glass bowl.

3. Mash the flesh with a fork and mix with the fresh lime juice.

4. Dice the rest of the avocado and gently mix it into the mashed avocado and lime mixture together with the finely chopped shallot or onion.

5. Season the guacamole carefully with salt and pepper.

Nutritional Facts per serving: Calories 106, Fat 9.8g, Carbohydrate 5.2g, Dietary Fiber 3.5g, Net Carbs 1.7g, Protein 1.0g.

ASPARAGUS IN A PROSCUITO BLANKET

Scrumptious, quick and just so simple for any time or meal of the day!

Makes 32 / Serves 8

INGREDIENTS:

32 small spears of fresh green asparagus

16 slices prosciutto ham

Olive oil

DIRECTIONS:

1. Thoroughly wash and dry the asparagus spears and snap off the root end if tough.

2. Cut the ham slices in half and wrap each around an asparagus spear. Make sure that the base is covered – the top may be left open.

3. In a large skillet heat a little olive oil and fry the wrapped asparagus for about 6 minutes turning carefully half way through.

4. Serve whilst still hot for whichever meal you prefer.

Nutritional Facts per serving of 4: Calories 91, Fat 4.7g, Carbohydrate 3.1g, Dietary Fiber 1.3g, Net Carbs 1.8g, Protein 9.8g.

BEEFY SCOTCH EGGS

Fancy a Scotch egg with a garlicky beefy coating? These are nice and filling, will make your mouth water and are very low in carbs!

Serves 6

INGREDIENTS:

1¾ pounds (795g) ground beef (not too lean)

6 large eggs

10 medium cloves of garlic (more or less to taste)

Paprika powder

DIRECTIONS:

1. Hard boil the eggs and when cool, carefully take off the shell.

2. Crush or very finely chop the garlic.

3. Mix the ground beef and garlic and divide it into 6 equal portions.

4. Flatten each portion of beef with your hands to form a flat, thin patty.

5. Mould each meat portion around an egg , gently forming it into a nicely rounded shape

6. Grill or bake the 'eggs' until cooked.

7. Serve the eggs cut in halves and sprinkled with paprika.

Nutritional Facts per egg: Calories 319, Fat 13.3g, Carbohydrate 0.7g, Dietary Fiber 0g, Net Carbs 0.7g, Protein 46.5g

CHICKEN AND BACON WRAPS

Oh my goodness! What is that delicious aroma emanating from the kitchen? Your guests will love these drool worthy treats.

Makes 30

INGREDIENTS:

1¼ pounds (568g) of chicken fillets

10 rashers of bacon

DIRECTIONS:

1. Pre-heat the oven to 375°F (191°C).

2. Prepare a baking tray by covering it with foil.

3. Cut the chicken fillet into 30 even sized pieces.

4. Cut each bacon rasher into 3.

5. Wrap a piece of bacon around each piece of chicken.

6. Place the chicken wraps onto the foil lined tray with the bacon seam down.

7. Place the tray on the middle rack of the oven and bake for about 25 minutes until brown and the bacon is crisp. You can turn the poppers half way through if you like.

8. Remove from the oven and drain the excess fat away on a paper towel.

9. Place a cocktail stick in each popper and serve hot.

Nutritional Facts per wrap: Calories 59, Fat 2.8g, Carbohydrate 0g, Dietary Fiber 0g, Net Carbs 0g, Protein 8.1g

PEPPERONI PIZZA

*A cheese base pizza which can be used to hold a variety of topping!
Pepperoni is used in this recipe but you could substitute with mushrooms,
ham, bacon, or whatever pizza toppings fit your nutritional goals.*

Serves 4

INGREDIENTS:

8 ounces (227g) mozzarella cheese, shredded

Garlic seasoning

Italian herb seasoning or herbs of your choice

2 ounces (57g) pepperoni, chopped

DIRECTIONS:

1. Heat a large non-stick skillet over a medium heat.

2. When hot, sprinkle in the cheese in an even layer to cover the
    base of the skillet.

3. Sprinkle over the garlic and herb seasonings as soon as the
    cheese starts to bubble as well as the pepperoni.

4. When the edges of the pizza begin to brown and it begins to
    loosen from the bottom of the skillet, slide the pizza out onto a
    serving plate.

5. Allow to stand for a minute or two to cool a little and to firm.

6. Cut into slices and enjoy.

*Nutritional Facts per portion: Calories 241, Fat 17.6g, Carbohydrate 2.2g,
Dietary Fiber 0g, Net Carbs 2.2g, Protein 17.9g.*

CRACKLED PORK

Pork scratching at its tasty best. You'll hear crunching in the silence as everyone tucks in!

Makes a good bowlful

INGREDIENTS:

2 pounds (908g) pork skin with a good fat layer

Fine sea salt

DIRECTIONS:

1. Preheat your oven to 325° F.

2. Line a baking sheet with parchment paper

3. Score the skin into thin strips but do not cut through. Use a sharp knife for this.

4. Rub the pork skin with plenty of salt

5. Place the skin, fat side down on the prepared baking sheet.

6. Place in the oven and cook for about 2 hours. (Beware, it will smell delicious!)

7. Check after an hour so that the pork is done to your desired level of crunchiness.

8. When ready remove from the oven, drain well and let it cool a bit.

9. Break along the scored lines and serve.

Nutritional Facts per 2 ounce (57g) portion: Calories 308, Fat 17.6, Carbohydrate 0g, Dietary Fiber 0g, Net Carbs 0g, Protein 34.8g.

GROUND BEEF JERKY

A fabulous jerky recipe that can be dried in a conventional oven. Munch away!

Makes 30 small pieces

INGREDIENTS:

3 pounds (1.35kg) ground beef

3 tbsp. salt

4 tbsp. light soy sauce

Olive oil

DIRECTIONS:

1. Mix the salt into the beef in a large bowl.

2. Oil the base of two large deep baking sheets with olive oil.

3. Press the beef into the sheets dividing it evenly between the two. It should not be more that ¼ inch (0.6cm) thick.

4. Brush the beef with the soy sauce before placing in a low oven, 150°F (66°C).

5. Leave to dry out overnight, or for about 10 hours, until the jerky is hard.

6. Pour off any fat that may have accumulated.

7. Turn out and cool. Break into manageable sized pieces.

8. Store in an airtight container in the fridge.

Nutritional Facts per piece: Calories 45, Fat 2.5g, Carbohydrate 0.2g, Dietary Fiber 0g, Net Carbs 0.2g, Protein 5.5g.

SAVORY STUFFED MUSHROOMS

A quick and easy appetiser. Add a little grated mozzarella cheese to the stuffing to give them an extra dimension. Enjoy!

Makes 24

INGREDIENTS:

24 small mushrooms

2 cups (308g) of canned crab, tuna or salmon

3 tbsp. finely snipped chives

3 cloves of garlic crushed

1 tsp. finely chopped thyme

1 tbsp. mayonnaise

Salt and pepper to taste

DIRECTIONS:

1. Clean the mushrooms gently and remove the stalks and ribs.
2. Pre-heat the oven to 375°F (191°C).
3. Lay the mushrooms out on a baking sheet, top down.
4. Drain fish and mix it together in a bowl with garlic and herbs.
5. Add the mayonnaise to moisten.
6. Season with salt and pepper to taste.
7. Using a teaspoon, fill the mushroom caps generously.
8. Bake in the hot oven for about 12 minutes.
9. Remove from the oven and place on a serving plate.
10. Serve whilst still warm.

Nutritional Facts per mushroom: Calories 31, Fat 1.4g, Carbohydrate 0.5g, Dietary Fiber 0g, Net Carbs 0.5g, Protein 4.0g.

ZINGY BACON EGGS

These eggs are excellent for a pre-dinner appetizer or lunch party. For extra zing, top with a cayenne pepper or a thin slice of pimento.

Makes 24 halves

INGREDIENTS:

12 large free range fresh eggs

8 rashers of bacon

½ cup (119ml) mayonnaise

1 tsp. mustard powder

1 tbsp. powdered cumin

Salt and freshly cracked black pepper

Paprika for dusting

DIRECTIONS:

1. Hard boil the eggs. Cool and peel.

2. Fry the bacon slices in a skillet until crisp and golden brown. Drain on kitchen paper.

3. Crumble the cooked bacon into a medium sized bowl.

4. Cut the eggs in half lengthways.

5. Scoop out yolks and add them to the bacon.

6. Add the mayonnaise, mustard and cumin into the bowl and mash everything well together.

7. Season to taste with salt and pepper.

8. Carefully fill the egg white halves with the bacon mixture.

9. Arrange on a plate and serve with a dusting of paprika.

Nutritional Facts per half egg: Calories 80, Fat 5.7g, Carbohydrate 1.6g, Dietary Fiber 0g, Net Carbs 1.6g, Protein 5.9g.

SAUSAGE AND EGG BURGERS

A yummy breakfast or lunch 'fix', especially on a Sunday!

Serves 4

INGREDIENTS:

1 pound (454g) pork breakfast sausage meat

4 large fresh farm eggs

2 tbsp. olive oil

2 tsp. fresh herbs – finely chopped

Salt and freshly ground black pepper

Hot chili sauce

DIRECTIONS:

1. In a small bowl mix the sausage meat with the herbs and season to taste.

2. Divide the sausage meat into 8 equal portions and with damp hands to prevent sticking, flatten each portion into a burger size patty.

3. Heat half of the olive oil in a pan over a medium heat and fry the prepared patties on both sides until cooked through.

4. Remove from the pan and drain on kitchen paper towel

5. Clean out the pan and heat once more with the rest of the oil.

6. Break the eggs in one by one and fry. They can be either sunny side up or flipped to your preference and cooked both sides.

7. Serve the eggs sandwiched between the sausage patties.

8. Serve topped with hot chili sauce.

Nutritional Facts per portion: Calories 419, Fat 35.2g, Carbohydrate 3.0g, Dietary Fiber 1.0 g, Net Carbs 2.0g, Protein 24.7g.

SALMON NIBBLES

These are perfect as an appetizer or as a snack in a lunch box, or perhaps place these nibbles around a mayo based dip for a party. Just remember to count the extra carbs for the dip.

Makes 32

INGREDIENTS:

2 pounds (908g) fresh salmon

8 ounces (227g) smoked salmon (not sugar smoked!)

2 fresh eggs

½ cup (48g) almond flour

2 tsp. soy sauce

1 tbsp. chopped green onions

2 cloves garlic, minced

Salt and pepper to taste

Oil for frying

Parsley to garnish

Lemon wedges

Cocktail sticks to serve

DIRECTIONS:

1. Skin and bone the salmon and dice finely.

2. Break up the smoked salmon into small pieces.

3. In a large bowl mix together the fish, eggs, almond flour, soy sauce, green onions, garlic, salt and pepper.

4. Form into 32 even sized nibbles.

5. Fry until golden brown in a skillet. Use only a little oil and do not overcook!

6. Remove from the skillet and drain on paper towel.

7. Place on a serving plate, put each one on a stick if you like and garnish with parsley.

8. Serve with lemon wedges.

Nutritional Facts per nibble: Calories 60, Fat 3.4g, Carbohydrate 0.2g, Dietary Fiber 0g, Net Carbs 0.2g, Protein 7.3g.

CHEESY PUFFS

Completely addictive and so easy to make! What more can you ask from a Keto snack?

Makes 60 small puffs

INGREDIENTS:

2 pounds (908g) frozen spinach, thawed and well drained

2 cups (192g) almond flour

4 ounces (113g) butter, melted

4 large fresh eggs

½ cup (50g) grated parmesan cheese

¾ cup (113g) feta cheese, crumbled

½ tsp. powdered nutmeg

3 cloves garlic, minced

3 green onions, minced

½ cup (118ml) heavy cream

Salt and pepper to taste

DIRECTIONS:

1. Ensure that the spinach is well thawed and as dry as you can get it. Use a paper towel if necessary to soak up any extra moisture.

2. Whizz all of the other ingredients in a blender or processor until well blended and smooth.

3. Add the spinach and whizz again until well mixed.

4. Place in the fridge to chill for 30 minutes.

5. Pre-heat the oven to 350°F (177°C).

6. Prepare 2 cookie sheets with parchment paper.

7.   Divide the cheesy spinach mixture into walnut sized pieces.

8.   Place each one on the prepared cookie sheets and bake until crisp for about 12 minutes. Do not over bake.

9.   Cool and serve.

Nutritional Facts per puff: Calories 42, Fat 3.7g, Carbohydrate 1.0g, Dietary Fiber 0g, Net Carbs 1.0g, Protein 1.7g.

MINI RICOTTA AND BACON MUFFINS

Munch these on your own if you dare or double the quantity and share!

Makes 12

INGREDIENTS:

10 ounces (284g) baby spinach, washed and drained

1 pound (454g) ricotta cheese

2 ounces (57g) toasted pine nuts, chopped

1 cup (100g) grated parmesan

½ cup (119ml) thick plain yogurt

2 large fresh eggs

7 ounces (198g) bacon

Salt and pepper to taste

DIRECTIONS:

1. Pre-heat the oven to 350°F (177°C).

2. Grease a 12 cup muffin pan with a little butter.

3. Boil some water in a large sauce pan and blanch the spinach for 30 seconds until just wilted.

4. Remove from the water, drain, dry and cool before chopping finely.

5. Finely chop the bacon or pulse in a processor.

6. In a large bowl mix all of the ingredients well together and spoon equally into the prepared muffin cups.

7. Bake in the pre-heated oven for 30 minutes until set and brown on the top.

Nutritional Facts per tart: Calories 228, Fat 16.2g, Carbohydrate 4.8g, Dietary Fiber 0.7g, Net Carbs 4.1 g, Protein 16.4g.

ZUCCHINI AND SALMON ROLLS

A versatile dish that can be made with salmon, tuna or even crab if you fancy it! These can be fiddly to make but well worth the effort.

Make 16 small rolls

INGREDIENTS:

2 medium zucchini

1 x 5 ounce (142g) can pink or red salmon

1 small avocado

2 tbsp. mayonnaise

1 small chili pepper, seeded and finely chopped

2 tsp. lime juice

Salt and pepper

Paprika or cayenne pepper to garnish

DIRECTIONS:

1. Slice the zucchini thinly lengthways using a potato peeler or a very sharp knife. This will give you ribbons of zucchini.

2. Cut each ribbon in half to give you 16 altogether.

3. Drain the salmon well and mix it with the mayonnaise, avocado flesh, chili pepper, lime juice and seasoning in a small bowl.

4. Place a small spoonful of the fish mixture at one end of each zucchini ribbon and roll it up. Use a tooth pick to secure the end if necessary.

5. Repeat with the other rolls and garnish with pepper.

6. Make these rolls just before serving as they do not keep.

Nutritional Facts per roll: Calories 51, Fat 3.7g, Carbohydrate 3.0g, Dietary Fiber 1.2g, Net Carbs 1.8g, Protein 2.3g.

CHICKEN AND CHEESE TACO

For that Mexican craving we all get once in a while! Try using other meats you have on hand and roll your own unique combinations!

Makes 4

INGREDIENTS:

2 cups (226g) grated mozzarella

2 chicken breasts, cooked and shredded

4 tbsp. sour cream

2 green onions, finely chopped

4 tsp. chili salsa

Salt and pepper

DIRECTIONS:

1. Pre-heat the oven to 350°F (177°C).

2. Line a baking tray with parchment.

3. Place 4 lots of cheese on the baking tray – ½ cup (56g) each.

4. Bake in the oven until melted and slightly crunchy.

5. Remove from the oven and leave until cool enough to handle.

6. Roll each one like a wrap, filled with equal amounts of chicken, sour cream, green onion and salsa.

7. Eat while still warm and crunchy!

Nutritional Facts per taco: Calories 367, Fat 20.4g, Carbohydrate 3.3g, Dietary Fiber 0g, Net Carbs 3.3g, Protein 40.6g.

CHEESY CHICKEN FINGERS

These fingers are ideal for lunch boxes or as picnic food. They are easily transportable and quite moreish.

Make 24

INGREDIENTS:

2 pounds (908g) chicken breast meat

1 cup (100g) grated parmesan cheese

2 tbsp. chopped herbs, thyme or parsley

Salt and pepper to taste

1 tsp. powdered chili pepper

4 ounces (113g) butter

4 cloves garlic, finely chopped

DIRECTIONS:

1. Pre-heat the oven to 350°F (177°C).

2. Grease a baking sheet with a little of the butter.

3. Place the remaining butter in a small saucepan with the chopped garlic and melt.

4. Leave for about 15 minutes for the garlic flavor to infuse.

5. Mix together the cheese, herbs, chili pepper and seasoning on a plate.

6. Cut the chicken breasts into 24 fingers and dip each into the butter and then the cheese mixture before placing on the baking sheet.

7. Place the tray in the oven and bake for 25 – minutes until cooked and golden brown.

8. Turn half way through the cooking time to ensure even browning.

9. Remove from the oven and eat warm or leave to cool completely before storing in the fridge.

Nutritional Facts per finger: Calories 121, Fat 6.6g, Carbohydrate 0.6g, Dietary Fiber 0g, Net Carbs 0.6g, Protein 14.2g.

CHINESE CHICKEN

Yummy chicken wings in a ginger soy sauce. Perfect on game day, or enjoyed as a party favorite. Excellent eaten warm or cold!

Makes 24

INGREDIENTS:

2 pounds (908g) chicken wings (24)

1 cup (237ml) soy sauce

½ cup (119ml) water

½ tsp. chili oil

1 tbsp. sesame oil

2 tbsp. lemon juice

3 cloves garlic, finely chopped

1 tbsp. fresh minced ginger

1 large stem lemon grass, bruised and finely minced

Liquid stevia extract (to taste)

DIRECTIONS:

1. Mix together all of the ingredients except the chicken wings in a large flat bottomed dish.

2. Wash and trim the chicken wings, dry and place in the dish with the marinade.

3. Coat well, cover with plastic wrap and refrigerate overnight.

4. Pre-heat the oven to 375°F (191°C).

5. Oil a roasting tin and place the drained wings on it.

6. Place in the hot oven and cook for 50 – 60 minutes turning 3 or 4 times during the cooking.

7. Remove from the oven and serve warm or cool down in the fridge to eat later.

Nutritional Facts per wing: Calories 85, Fat 3.5g, Carbohydrate 1.2g, Dietary Fiber 0g, Net Carbs 1.2g, Protein 11.7g.

CHEDDAR PANCAKES

Pancakes on Keto? Praise the heavens! Try these with some heavy cream and a couple of low GI berries, like strawberries or blueberries.

Makes 8

INGREDIENTS:

4 large eggs, whites only

2 cups (192g) almond meal

4 ounces (113g) Cheddar cheese, grated

1 tbsp. green onion, finely chopped

2 cloves garlic, finely chopped

1 tsp. baking powder

4 tbsp. olive oil

½ cup (119ml) water

Oil to grease a skillet

DIRECTIONS:

1. Mix all of the ingredients together in a large bowl.

2. Pre-heat a skillet to medium-high, non-stick if you have one.

3. Pour in a little oil to just cover the bottom of the skillet.

4. Using a soup ladle pour one eighth of the mixture into the skillet.

5. Cook for about a minute until bubbles rise to the surface and start to pop.

6. Turn with a spatula and cook the other side for about a minute.

7. Serve warm with butter.

Nutritional Facts per pancake: Calories 319, Fat 28.1g, Carbohydrate 5.9g, Dietary Fiber 3.0g, Net Carbs 2.9g, Protein 12.4g.

PEPPERONI MUFFINS À LA CHEESE

Italian flavors of pepperoni, cheese and seasoning create tasty morsels!

Makes 12

INGREDIENTS:

3 ounces (85g) ground flax seed

1½ tsp. baking powder

2 tbsp. Italian seasoning

8 fresh eggs, lightly beaten

8 ounces (227g) mozzarella cheese, shredded

½ cup (50g) grated parmesan cheese

7 ounces (198g) pepperoni, finely diced

Salt and pepper to taste

DIRECTIONS:

1. Pre-heat the oven to 375°F (191°C).

2. Grease 12 muffin cups well.

3. Mix together the flax seed, baking powder, Italian seasoning and salt and pepper in a large bowl.

4. Stir in the beaten egg followed by the cheeses and pepperoni.

5. Leave the mixture to rest for about 10 minutes before stirring and spooning equally among the prepared muffin cups.

6. Place in the pre-heated oven and bake until risen and golden – about 20 minutes.

7. Remove from the oven and cool a little on a wire rack.

8. Serve warm.

Nutritional Facts per muffin: Calories 254, Fat 19.1g, Carbohydrate 4.3g, Dietary Fiber 2.0g, Net Carbs 2.3g, Protein 16.8g.

SMOKED SALMON MAKI

Sushi rolls without the rice and nori. You'll need wax paper for this one to help with the roll. These are fantastic, and delicious indeed!

Makes 12

INGREDIENTS:

12 ounces (340g) smoked salmon

2 Lebanese cucumbers (small cucumbers)

1 avocado

7 ounces (198g) cream cheese

Wasabi to taste

¼ cup (37.5g) sesame seeds

½ cup (119ml) soy sauce for dipping

Pickled ginger to serve

DIRECTIONS:

1. Beat the cream cheese with a little wasabi paste until smooth and soft enough to spread.

2. Lay out the smoked salmon on waxed paper so that it slightly overlaps into two 6 inch (15cm) squares.

3. Spread each layer with cream cheese.

4. Peel the avocado and cut into strips.

5. Cut the cucumber into thin strips, leave the skin on.

6. Lay the avocado strips and cucumber along one side of each salmon layer.

7. Using the waxed paper to help you, start rolling up the salmon from the end where the vegetables are - Swiss roll style!

8. When rolled up roll in sesame seeds and leave to 'set for 30 minutes in the refrigerator.

9. Use a sharp knife to cut each roll into 6 x 1 inch (2.5cm) portions. Lay on a plate cut side up.

10. Serve with soy sauce to dip and pickled ginger to accompany each mouthful.

Nutritional Facts per maki: Calories 156, Fat 11.8g, Carbohydrate 5.4g, Dietary Fiber 1.9g, Net Carbs 4.1g, Protein 8.2g.

TUNA NORI ROLLS

Spicy rolls with tuna and raw veggies reminiscent of a Japanese delight.

Makes 12

INGREDIENTS:

2 sheets nori (dried seaweed)

2 cans tuna fish

4 tbsp. mayonnaise

4 tbsp. parsley, finely chopped

1 medium ripe avocado, peeled and cut into sticks

¼ red sweet bell pepper, finely sliced

Chili sauce

DIRECTIONS:

1. Mix together the tuna, mayonnaise and parsley in a small bowl.

2. Lay out the nori with the shiny side down on a sushi mat if you have one. If not, plastic wrap works well!

3. Spread the tuna mixture over the bottom half of each nori sheet.

4. Place the avocado and pepper slices alongside the tuna on the nori sheet.

5. Start rolling from the vegetable end – like a Swiss roll. Use the sushi mat or plastic wrap to help you. Press firmly as you go so that the nori sticks together.

6. With a very sharp knife cut each roll into 6 even sized pieces.

7. Serve with a little chili sauce on the top of each portion.

Nutritional Facts per roll: Calories 118, Fat 7.6g, Carbohydrate 2.8g, Dietary Fiber 1.4g, Net Carbs 1.4g, Protein 9.4g.

MUSHROOMS WITH NUT STUFFING

Stuffed broiled mushrooms with a nutty filling and melted cheese on top – what could be more inviting?

Makes 12

INGREDIENTS:

12 mushroom caps – 2 inches (5cm) in diameter

¾ cup (75g) walnut or pecan pieces

1 cup (60g) chopped parsley

3 cloves garlic, finely chopped

¼ cup (25g) grated parmesan cheese

¼ cup (59ml) olive oil

12 small slices mozzarella cheese

Salt and pepper to taste

DIRECTIONS:

1. Lay the mushroom cups on a non-stick broiler pan – top side down.

2. Place the nuts, parsley, garlic and parmesan in a processor or liquidiser and pulse until crumbly.

3. Add the olive oil and pulse until a rough paste is formed.

4. Spoon the nut mixture among the mushroom caps and top each with a slice of mozzarella cheese.

5. Place under a hot broiler for 6 – 8 minutes until cooked through and the cheese is bubbling.

6. Serve warm.

Nutritional Facts per mushroom: Calories 160, Fat 14.1g, Carbohydrate 2.2g, Dietary Fiber 1.0g, Net Carbs 1.2g, Protein 8.2g.

CHICKEN AND VEGETABLE KEBABS

Lemony chicken and bell peppers grilled to perfection – great cooked over a barbeque! Add any other vegetables you wish, carbs permitting.

Makes 8 skewers

INGREDIENTS:

2 pounds (908g) chicken breast, skinned and boned

1 red bell pepper

1 green bell pepper

¾ cup (178ml) olive oil

1 lemon, zested and juiced

3 cloves garlic, crushed

1 tbsp. parsley, finely chopped

Salt and pepper to taste

DIRECTIONS:

1. Soak 8 wooden kebab skewers in water.

2. Chop the chicken breasts into cubes of about 1 inch (2.5cm).

3. Mix together ¼ cup olive oil (59ml), lemon zest, garlic, chopped parsley and seasonings.

4. Add the chopped chicken and stir to coat. Cover and leave to marinade in the fridge overnight.

5. De-seed and chop the peppers into 1 inch (2.5cm) 'squares'. Set aside.

6. Whisk together the remaining olive oil, the lemon juice and seasoning.

7. Turn on the broiler to a medium heat or fire up the barbeque.

8. Thread the chicken and peppers onto soaked skewers.

9. Brush with the olive oil and lemon mixture and broil until cooked – about 10 minutes. The chicken will be opaque and the peppers soft and brown around the edges.

10. Place on a serving plate and eat while warm.

Nutritional Facts per kebab: Calories 391, Fat 27.4g, Carbohydrate 2.9g, Dietary Fiber 0.9g, Net Carbs 2.0g, Protein 33.3g.

HERBY MUSHROOM SLICE

Slices of mushroom and herb which are very versatile from snack to light lunch or even a starter for a dinner party!

Makes 10 slices

INGREDIENTS:

10 ounces (284g) sautéed mushrooms, cooked weight

1 small onion, finely chopped

5 ounces (142g) Cheddar cheese, grated

3 large fresh eggs, separated

¼ cup (36g) chopped dill

¼ cup (15g) chopped parsley

1 tbsp. chopped thyme

2 tbsp. olive oil

Salt and pepper to taste

DIRECTIONS:

1. Preheat the oven to 400°F (204°C).

2. Line a roasting tin with parchment or use a non-stick tin.

3. Place a skillet over a medium heat and fry the onion in the oil for a couple of minutes.

4. Add the mushroom and herbs and take off the heat to cool a little.

5. When cool stir in the egg yolks and the cheese. Season to taste.

6. Beat the egg whites until they form soft peaks and then gently fold them into the mushroom mixture.

7. Spoon the mixture into the prepared tin and bake for 25 minutes until brown.

8.   Remove from the oven and cool in the tin.

9.   Cut into slices.

10. Serve warm or chilled

Nutritional Facts per slice: Calories 144, Fat 11.8g, Carbohydrate 3.7g, Dietary Fiber 1.1g, Net Carbs 2.6g, Protein 6.7g.

SMOKED TROUT PÂTÉ CUCUMBER ROUNDS

A tasty pâté which could be enjoyed on Keto crackers as an alternative to slices of cucumber.

Makes 20

INGREDIENTS:

4 ounces (113g) smoked trout, skinned and boned

3 ounces (85g) cream cheese

2 tbsp. onion, grated

2 tbsp. lemon juice, freshly squeezed

½ tsp. Worcestershire sauce

½ tsp. freshly ground black pepper

Tabasco to taste

Chopped chives to garnish

1 small cucumber, cut into 20 x ¼ inch (0.6cm) slices

DIRECTIONS:

1. Place all of the ingredients except the chives into a processor or blender.

2. Pulse until light and smooth. Add some more lemon juice or a little water if the mixture is too thick.

3. Place spoonfuls on the cucumber slices and serve sprinkled with chives.

Nutritional Facts per round: Calories 29, Fat 2.0g, Carbohydrate 0.8g, Dietary Fiber 0g, Net Carbs 0.8g, Protein 2.0g.

CHEESY WAFFLES

Use a waffle maker or a hot flat griddle plate for this cheesy treat.

Makes 12

INGREDIENTS:

2 cups (290g) cauliflower crumbs, made in a processor

2 cups (226g) grated mozzarella cheese

½ cup (50g) grated parmesan

4 fresh eggs

2 tsp. garlic powder

2 tsp. onion powder

1 tsp. freshly ground black pepper

2 tbsp. chopped chives

Salt to taste

Butter for greasing

DIRECTIONS:

1. Mix all of the ingredients together in a large bowl.

2. Pre-heat a waffle maker according to instructions.

3. Add a soup ladle of batter into the hot waffle maker and cook for about 5 minutes.

4. If the waffle sticks – cook for a little longer.

5. Remove and allow to cool. Store in the fridge.

6. If using a hot griddle – grease with a little butter and pour tablespoons of the batter onto it.

7. After a couple of minutes turn and cook the other side.

Nutritional Facts per waffle: Calories 112, Fat 7.3g, Carbohydrate 2.3g, Dietary Fiber 0.6g, Net Carbs 1.7g, Protein 8.9g.

BACON ROLL

Hot Keto style sushi with everyone's favorite!

Makes 12 small rolls

INGREDIENTS:

1 pound (454g) smoky bacon slices

4 ounces (113g) mozzarella cheese, shredded

1 tsp. hot chili sauce

DIRECTIONS:

1. Pre-heat the oven to 400°F (204°C).

2. Lay the bacon slices on a baking tray and bake until well browned but not crisp – about 15 minutes.

3. Drain any excess fat by blotting with paper towels and lay the bacon out into a 'mat' with the edges of each slice overlapping the one next to it.

4. Sprinkle with the grated cheese and the hot sauce.

5. Roll up from one end like a sushi roll and place back on the baking tray.

6. Put the roll back into the oven for 5 – 10 minutes or so to melt the cheese.

7. Remove from the oven and place on a chopping board.

8. Slice into 12 rolls.

9. Serve hot.

Nutritional Facts per portion: Calories 99, Fat 7.3g, Carbohydrate 0.4g, Dietary Fiber 0g, Net Carbs 0.4g, Protein 7.1g.

CAULIFLOWER NUGGETS

These are crispy and tasty if eaten straight after cooking. Have your guests ready and waiting for this treat!

Makes 40

INGREDIENTS:

1 cauliflower, medium sized

2 tbsp. heavy cream

2 tbsp. butter

½ cup (57g) strong Cheddar cheese, grated

4 fresh eggs, whites only

Salt and pepper to taste

Paprika to sprinkle

DIRECTIONS:

1. Break the cauliflower into florets and cook in a little salted water until still slightly crisp. Drain well.

2. Cool a little and then place in a blender with the butter and the cram and pulse to a porridge like consistency.

3. Season with salt and pepper, turn into a large bowl and allow to cool.

4. Whip the egg whites until stiff and fold into the cold cauliflower mixture.

5. Place in the fridge for 30 minutes to cool once more.

6. While the cauliflower is cooling pre-heat the oven to 375°F (191°C).

7. Grease 2 large cookie sheets.

8. Place spoonfuls of the cauliflower mixture on the cookie sheets.

9. Bake in the hot oven for 15 – 40 minutes until brown and crispy.

10. Remove from the oven, sprinkle with paprika and serve at once!

Nutritional Facts per nugget: Calories 23, Fat 1.8g, Carbohydrate 0.9g, Dietary Fiber 0g, Net Carbs 0.9g, Protein 1.2g

TUNA EGGS

Stuffed eggs are an all-time favorite. Try other tinned fish instead of tuna, or finely chopped ham. Add a few drops of Tabasco sauce if you would like to add some extra heat!

Makes 12 halves

INGREDIENTS:

6 large fresh eggs, hard boiled

6 ounce (170g) can tuna in oil, drained

½ cup (119ml) mayonnaise

1 small onion, minced

1 small stick celery, minced

¼ tsp. hot English mustard

Salt and pepper to taste

Cayenne pepper to dust

DIRECTIONS:

1. Peel the eggs and slice in half, lengthways.

2. Remove the yolks with a teaspoon and place them in a small bowl with the flaked tuna, mayonnaise, onion, celery and mustard.

3. Mix very well together and season to taste.

4. Place spoonfuls of the tuna mixture back into the egg white shells, arrange on a plate and dust with cayenne.

Nutritional Facts per half egg: Calories 106, Fat 6.9g, Carbohydrate 3.4g Dietary Fiber 0g, Net Carbs 3.4g, Protein 7.4g.

SEEDED CRACKERS

Delicious nutty tasting crackers which keep well in an airtight tin or in the freezer. Use with dips and spreads or just on their own for crunchy munchie goodness.

Makes 48

INGREDIENTS:

1½ cups (144g) almond flour

3 tsp. granulated sugar substitute

2 fresh eggs, whites only

¾ tsp. salt

¼ tsp. garlic powder

2 tbsp. sesame seeds

2 ounces (57g) softened butter

DIRECTIONS:

1. Place all of the ingredients into a medium sized bowl and mix thoroughly together.

2. Roll into a sausage shape, about 1 inch (2.5cm) in diameter, and place in plastic wrap.

3. Refrigerate for 45 minutes to chill.

4. Pre-heat the oven to 350°F (177°C).

5. Line several baking sheets with parchment paper. (Bake in batches if you do not have enough sheets)

6. Remove the chilled dough and using a very sharp knife cut off thin slices and place them on the prepared baking sheets.

7. If your kitchen is warm, put the dough back in the fridge to chill between baking batches.

8. Dampen a finger with a little water and press each round down so it is as thin as you can make it.

9. Prick the rounds with a fork and bake for 12 – 15 minutes until brown.

10. Leave to cool on the baking sheets for a moment before removing to a cooling rack.

Nutritional Facts per cracker: Calories 34, Fat 3.0g, Carbohydrate 0.7g, Dietary Fiber 0.4g, Net Carbs 0.3g, Protein 1.1g.

ZUCCHINI CRISPS

These delicious Keto crisps are perfect to dip or eat as they are!

Makes a large bowl full – serves 6

INGREDIENTS:

6 large zucchini, about 6 inches (15cm) each

Oil for deep frying

Salt to sprinkle

DIRECTIONS:

1. Top and tail the zucchini and slice into thin rounds.

2. Heat some oil in a deep fat fryer and fry the zucchini rounds in batches until golden and crisp, turning as they fry.

3. Remove from the oil and drain well on paper towel.

4. Place in a serving bowl and sprinkle with salt.

5. Serve!

Nutritional Facts per portion: Calories 127, Fat 9.4, Carbohydrate 10.8g, Dietary Fiber 3.5g, Net Carbs 7.3g, Protein 3.9g

PORTUGUESE PERI PERI CHICKEN BITES

Baked chicken bites with lemon and chili are such a zesty combination.

Serves 6

INGREDIENTS:

2 pounds (908g) chicken breasts, boned and skinned

3 lemons, juiced

¼ cup (59ml) olive oil

3 cloves garlic, crushed

1 small onion, grated

2 tsp. chili powder (to taste)

Salt and pepper

DIRECTIONS:

1. Mix together the garlic, lemon juice and the olive oil.

2. Add the onion and chili powder. Set aside.

3. Cut the chicken breast up into 1 inch (2.5cm) cubes.

4. Place in the lemon marinade and refrigerate for 1 hour.

5. Pre-heat the oven to 350°F (177°C).

6. Remove the chicken from the marinade and place in an ovenproof dish in a single layer.

7. Bake for 15 – 20 minutes until cooked, basting with extra marinade half way through the cooking time.

8. Remove from the oven, sprinkle with salt and pepper and serve.

Nutritional Facts per portion: Calories 287, Fat 20.5g, Carbohydrate 4.8g, Dietary Fiber 1.4g, Net Carbs 3.4g, Protein 44.4g.

CHORIZO AND SHRIMP STICKS

Sausage and shrimp? They come together nicely to make these party nibbles with a Spanish flavor. So tasty!

Makes approximately 60

INGREDIENTS:

1 pound (454g) medium shrimps

1 pound (454g) Spanish chorizo sausage

2 tsp. crushed fresh garlic

1 tsp. dried marjoram

2 tbsp. sherry vinegar

2 tbsp. dry sherry

½ cup (119ml) olive oil

4 tbsp. chopped parsley

60 wooden tooth picks

Extra olive oil for frying

DIRECTIONS:

1. Peel, de-vein and clean the shrimp.

2. Combine the vinegar, sherry, oil, garlic a marjoram in a bowl and leave in the fridge for an hour for the flavors to mingle.

3. While the marinade is resting slice the chorizo into bite sized pieces – you should try to get 60.

4. Place the chorizo and the shrimp into the marinade so that each piece is thoroughly coated.

5. Thread 1 shrimp and 1 piece of sausage onto each stick.

6. Heat a little oil in a skillet over a medium high heat.

7. Place a few of the sticks into the skillet and cook until the chorizo is slightly brown and the shrimp nicely pink! Just a few

minutes!

8. Remove the sticks and drain on paper towel.

9. Keep warm and serve sprinkled with parsley.

10. These may also be cooked in a medium oven for about 10 minutes if you prefer.

Nutritional Facts per snack: Calories 52, Fat 4.1g, Carbohydrate 0.2g, Dietary Fiber 0g, Net Carbs 0.2g, Protein 3.5g.

MEXICAN TURKEY BITES

Yummy turkey with veggies and chili! Eat as they are or with a tangy yogurt dip.

Makes 36 bites

INGREDIENTS:

3 pounds (1.35kg) raw turkey, ground

1 large onion, finely chopped

3 medium tomatoes, skinned and finely chopped

1 small red bell pepper, finely chopped

⅓ cup (37g) flaxseed meal

2 fresh jalapeno peppers, finely chopped

1 tbsp. salt

1 tsp. pepper

Few drops Tabasco

DIRECTIONS:

1. Pre-heat the oven to 375°F (191°C).

2. Grease 2 baking sheets.

3. Mix all of the ingredients together in a large bowl until well combined.

4. Divide the mixture into 36 even sized portions and roll each into a ball. Flatten each ball slightly and place on the prepared baking sheets.

5. Bake for 25 – 30 minutes until golden and cooked through.

6. Serve hot or cold!

Nutritional Facts per bite: Calories 79, Fat 2.7g, Carbohydrate 1.6g, Dietary Fiber 0.9g, Net Carbs 0.7g, Protein 11.5g

are perfect to keep on hand for that hunger pang

INGREDIENTS:

1 cup (112g) coconut flour

1 cup (96g) almond flour

4 tsp. baking powder

1 tsp. garlic powder

1 tsp. onion powder

1 tsp. salt

1½ cups (170g) grated Cheddar cheese

6 large fresh eggs

1 cup (237ml) sour cream

½ cup (119ml) thick plain yogurt

½ cup (119ml) butter, melted

Freshly ground black pepper to taste

DIRECTIONS:

1. Pre-heat the oven to 375°F (191°C).

2. Cover 2 baking sheets with parchment paper.

3. In a large bowl mix together the flours, baking powder, garlic, onion and salt.

4. Stir in 1 cup (113g) of the grated Cheddar cheese.

5. In a separate bowl mix together the eggs, cream, yogurt and melted butter.

6. Mix the wet ingredients into the dry ingredients and combine well.

7. Using a dessert spoon drop the mixture onto the prepared sheets leaving a space in-between the biscuits as they spread and rise.

8. Sprinkle the remaining cheese on top of the biscuits.

9. Bake for 20 – 25 minutes until firm and turning brown.

10. Remove from the oven and cool on the sheets for a few minutes before transferring to a cooling rack.

Nutritional Facts per biscuit: Calories 133, Fat 10.6g, Carbohydrate 4.4g, Dietary Fiber 1.8g, Net Carbs 2.6g, Protein 4.9g.

SOUVLAKIA – GREEK LAMB MORSELS

A taste of the Mediterranean and sunshine.

Serves 12

INGREDIENTS:

6 pounds (2.7kg) lamb meat from the leg

1½ (356ml) cups olive oil

1 cup (237ml) dry red wine

½ cup (119ml) fresh lemon juice

4 cloves garlic, minced

4 bay leaves, torn

3 tbsp. fresh oregano, finely chopped

Salt and pepper to taste

DIRECTIONS:

1. Cut up the lamb into 1 inch (2.5cm) cubes.

2. Mix all of the other ingredients together in a large bowl.

3. Add lamb, cover and place in the fridge to marinade overnight.

4. Soak 12 large or 24 small wooden skewers in water.

5. Remove the lamb from the marinade with a slotted spoon and set aside. Remove the torn bay leaves and discard.

6. Place the marinade in a small saucepan and reduce over a medium heat by half – this will be used to baste the meat.

7. Thread the lamb onto the skewers, do not crowd the pieces.

8. Grill over a medium barbeque or under a broiler for about 20 minutes, turning and basting as the meat cooks.

Nutritional Facts per portion: Calories 707, Fat 59.8g, Carbohydrate 1.8g, Dietary Fiber 0.5g, Net Carbs 1.3g, Protein 38.4g.

SAUSAGE AND CHEESE MUNCHIES

These crunchy biscuits are made from whey protein. Use an unflavored, unsweetened whey for this recipe.

Makes 16

INGREDIENTS:

1½ cups (145g) plain low carbohydrate whey protein

2 cups (226g) grated Cheddar cheese

8 ounces (227g) pork sausage meat, cooked and crumbled

4 tsp. baking powder

½ tsp. baking soda

4 tbsp. almond flour

2 tbsp. oat fibre

1 tsp. garlic powder

2 fresh eggs, beaten

½ cup (119ml) melted butter

6 tbsp. heavy cream

DIRECTIONS:

1. Pre-heat the oven to 300°F (149°C).

2. Grease 16 muffin cups.

3. Mix together the melted butter, cream and beaten eggs in a large bowl.

4. Add the cooked sausage and cheese and stir well.

5. In a separate bowl mix together all of the dry ingredients and stir into the egg mixture, well.

6. Place about 3 tablespoons of mixture into each prepared muffin cup. Top up the cups if you have extra mixture.

7. Bake in the hot oven for about 12 minutes until set and risen.

8. Remove from the oven and let sit for a few minutes before turning out onto a cake rack to cool.

Nutritional Facts per munchie: Calories 253, Fat 19.1g, Carbohydrate 4.8g, Dietary Fiber 1.1g, Net Carbs 3.7g, Protein 16.1g.

CHEESE AND BACON PEPPER BOMBS

Your mouth will be left dancing after you have tasted these little bombs! They're easy to make and so worth making an extra quantity.

Make 8

INGREDIENTS:

8 jalapeno peppers

6 ounces (170g) full fat cream cheese

8 small strips bacon, cooked, crisped and finely chopped

8 small strips bacon for wrapping

2 tsp. garlic powder

1 tsp. chili powder

DIRECTIONS:

1. Pre-heat the oven to 350°F (177°C).

2. Have ready a small roasting tin with a wire rack in it.

3. Carefully slice the peppers down one side and remove the seeds. Try to leave the stem on.

4. In a small bowl mix together the cream cheese, bacon bits and the flavorings.

5. Spoon this mixture equally among the 8 peppers and wrap each pepper in a raw bacon strip.

6. Place the filled peppers on a wire rack in the roasting tin and place in the hot oven.

7. Bake for about 8 – 10 minutes until soft. Do not let your peppers collapse!

Nutritional Facts per bomb: Calories 289, Fat 23.6g, Carbohydrate 2.8g, Dietary Fiber 0.7g, Net Carbs 2.1g, Protein 16.1g.

OOPSIE ROLLS

Here's a popular recipe for flour free rolls. Try other flavors of cream cheese – herb, smoked salmon and chili flavors are good. These are easy enough to make a larger quantity, and store in an airtight container.

Makes 6

INGREDIENTS:

3 large fresh eggs, separated

2 tsp. powdered sugar substitute

1 pinch salt

1 pinch cream of tartar

3 ounces (85g) plain cream cheese

DIRECTIONS:

1. Pre-heat the oven to 300°F (149°C).

2. Cover a baking sheet with parchment paper.

3. Combine the egg yolks, sugar substitute, salt and cream cheese in a bowl. Beat well together – use a mixer if you have one.

4. Whisk together the egg whites and the cream of tartar until soft peaks.

5. Fold the whites carefully into the yolk mixture with a metal spoon. DO NOT BEAT.

6. Spoon the mixture onto the prepared baking sheet. Flatten each roll a little with the bake of a spoon.

7. Bake for about 30 minutes until cooked through but still soft.

8. Remove from the oven and cool on a wire rack.

Nutritional Facts per roll: Calories 84, Fat 6.8g, Carbohydrate 1.3g, Dietary Fiber 0g, Net Carbs 1.3g, Protein 4.2g.

PORK SAUSAGE BURGERS

Try these delicious 'burgers' served with an Oopsie roll, flavorful patty and lots of cheese! Top with chili sauce or a sugar free tomato sauce to taste.

Serves 4

INGREDIENTS:

4 pork sausages, skinned

4 eggs

4 ounces (113g) Cheddar cheese, sliced

4 Oopsie rolls *(see recipe from previous page)*

DIRECTIONS:

1. Form the sausage meat into 4 patties and fry until cooked in a little oil.

2. Fry the eggs until cooked as you like them!

3. Cut the rolls in half and top the bottom half of each with a patty, topped with and egg and then a generous portion of cheese.

4. Put the top back on each bun and serve.

Nutritional Facts (including Oopsie roll): Calories 435, Fat 34.8g, Carbohydrate 2.8g, Dietary Fiber 0g, Net Carbs 5.4g, Protein 26.5g.

CRISPY ONION RINGS

Deliciously crispy onion rings that you just have to try! These are a little higher in carbs so be careful with those serving sizes!

Serves 6

INGREDIENTS:

2 large yellow onions, peeled, sliced and ringed

2 tbsp. fresh thyme, finely chopped

1½ cups (144g) almond meal

½ tsp. salt

½ tsp. pepper

½ tsp. garlic powder

½ tsp. paprika

2 fresh eggs

DIRECTIONS:

1. Pre-heat the oven to 350°F (177°C).

2. Prepare 2 baking sheets with parchment paper.

3. Mix all of the dry ingredients, except the onion rings in a large bowl.

4. Beat the eggs in a separate bowl.

5. Dip each onion ring into the egg and then the dry mixture.

6. Shake off any extra coating and then place on the prepared baking sheets.

7. Bake for 20 – 25 minutes turning the rings half way through the baking time.

Nutritional Facts per portion: Calories 87, Fat 5.1g, Carbohydrate 7.2g, Dietary Fiber 2.2g, Net Carbs 5.0g, Protein 3.9g.

PIZZA WITH A CHICKEN CRUST

A nice change from the usual cauliflower pizza base used in Keto recipes!

Makes 8 slices

INGREDIENTS:

7 ounces (198g) chicken breast meat, ground

7 ounces (198g) mozzarella cheese, grated

1 tsp. garlic salt

1 tsp. dried basil

4 tbsp. pizza topping sauce

4 ounces (113g) Cheddar cheese, grated

12 slices pepperoni

Fresh basil leaves

DIRECTIONS:

1. Pre-heat the oven to 450°F (232°C).

2. Have ready a 12 inch (30cm) pizza pan lined with parchment.

3. Mix the chicken, cheese, garlic salt and dried basil together.

4. Spread into the pizza pan in an even layer and bake in the pre-heated oven for 10 – 12 minutes.

5. Remove from the oven and cool a little before adding the topping of sauce, Cheddar cheese and pepperoni.

6. Once the topping is one replace in the hot oven and cook for 5 – 7 minutes until hot and bubbly.

7. Remove from the oven and top with some torn basil leaves.

8. Cut and serve.

Nutritional Facts per slice: Calories 228, Fat 14.6g, Carbohydrate 3.0g, Dietary Fiber 0g, Net Carbs 3.0g, Protein 20.2g.

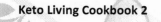

SWEET
TEMPTATIONS

COCO-NUT COOKIES

Enjoy this no-bake adventurous cookie with a mouth-watering combination of cocoa, peanut butter and coconut!

Makes 24

INGREDIENTS:

2 tbsp. butter

6 tbsp. heavy cream

4 tsp. cocoa

1½ tsp. liquid stevia extract (adjust to taste)

2 tbsp. smooth peanut butter

4 tbsp. rolled oats

½ cup (47g) unsweetened coconut, shredded

½ cup (56g) coconut flour

½ tsp. vanilla extract

DIRECTIONS:

1. Place the butter, heavy cream, cocoa and liquid sweetener in a small saucepan and place over a medium heat.

2. Bring gently to the boil while stirring to mix all of the ingredients well together. Boil for 1 minute – continue to stir.

3. Add the peanut butter to the hot mixture and then stir in the rest of the ingredients.

4. Drop small spoonfuls onto a baking sheet covered with waxed paper. Press the mounds together with your fingers if necessary.

5. Cool. Place in the refrigerator until firm.

Nutritional Facts per cookie: Calories 50, Fat 3.9g, Carbohydrate 2.7g, Dietary Fiber 1.2g, Net Carbs 1.5g, Protein 1.0g.

WALNUT CHOCOLATE NIBBLES

A perfect treat for the whole family, nutritious and great tasting!

Makes 60

INGREDIENTS:

¾ cup (178ml) coconut oil

¾ cup (150g) granulated sugar substitute

½ cup (43g) unsweetened cocoa powder

1 cup (112g) coconut flour

1 tbsp. ground cinnamon

4 large fresh eggs, beaten

3½ ounces (99g) dark chocolate (85% cocoa solids)

60 walnut halves

DIRECTIONS:

1. Warm the coconut oil to melt it.

2. Whisk in the beaten eggs and the sugar substitute.

3. Stir in the cocoa, cinnamon and the coconut flour.

4. Knead if necessary to remove any lumps, place in plastic wrap and refrigerate for an hour.

5. Pre-heat the oven to 350°F (177°C).

6. Line a couple of baking sheets with parchment paper.

7. Remove the dough from the fridge and roll it out between 2 sheets of parchment paper to a thickness of about ¼ inch (0.6cm).

8. Remove the top layer of parchment and cut out 2 inch (5cm) rounds of dough using a cookie cutter.

9. Lift each one off the bottom parchment and place on the prepared cookie sheets.

10. Gather up any dough not cut and roll out as before. Continue in this way until all of the dough has been used up.

11. Place the filled cookie sheets in the oven and bake for 8 – 10 minutes, making sure they do not burn.

12. If you do not have enough cookie sheets then bake a second batch.

13. Let the cookies cool completely before finishing them off.

14. Melt the dark chocolate in a small bowl over a pan of simmering water.

15. Using a small spoon put dollops of chocolate on the top of each cookie followed by a walnut half.

16. Leave to set before serving.

Nutritional Facts per nibble: Calories 63, Fat 5.4g, Carbohydrate 2.4g, Dietary Fiber 1.3g, Net Carbs 1.1g, Protein 1.5g.

SALTY CHOCOLATE BARK

Sweet or savory? Well it could be both – why not? Try this with some chili powder instead of salt, or use both if you like.

Makes 20 pieces

INGREDIENTS:

12 ounces (340g) dark chocolate (70% cocoa solids or higher)

Coarse crystal salt

4 ounces (113g) blanched almonds, chopped

DIRECTIONS:

1.   Line a cookie sheet that has edges with parchment paper.

2.   Chop up the chocolate, or coarsely grate it into a ceramic bowl.

3.   Place the bowl over a pan of simmering water and gently melt the chocolate, stirring from time to time.

4.   Remove the bowl from the heat and continue stirring until the chocolate is smooth and shiny. If adding chili powder, do so here.

5.   Pour the chocolate into the prepared cookie sheet and level it out using a flat bladed knife.

6.   While still warm sprinkle on the salt and the nuts pressing both in carefully with the back of a spoon.

7.   Refrigerate for 30 minutes until solid.

8.   Remove from the fridge and the cookie sheet and break into 20 even sized pieces.

9.   Store in a cool place.

Nutritional Facts per portion: Calories 137, Fat 10.6g, Carbohydrate 8.6g, Dietary Fiber 2.4g, Net Carbs 6.2g, Protein 2.5g.

CHOCOLATE BROWNIES

Who doesn't love an indulgent chocolate brownie? Save up a few carbs in your daily allowance to enjoy a few of these!

Makes 36

INGREDIENTS:

1 cup (96g) almond flour

½ cup (56g) coconut flour

1 scoop whey protein powder (chocolate flavor)

1 cup (86g) cocoa powder, unsweetened

1 cup (200g) granulated sugar substitute

1 tbsp. baking powder

4 ounces (113g) dark chocolate (80% cocoa solids)

3 large fresh eggs, beaten

½ cup (118ml) heavy cream

¼ cup (59ml) butter, unsalted

½ cup (119ml) cold water

2 tsp. vanilla extract

DIRECTIONS:

1. Pre-heat the oven to 325°F (163°C).

2. Line a 12 x 12 inch (30 x 30cm) pan with parchment.

3. Mix together the flours, whey protein, sugar substitute and baking powder in a medium sized bowl.

4. Warm together the chocolate, water, cream, butter and cocoa.

5. Stir well and then allow to cool.

6. Mix in the vanilla extract.

7. Beat the eggs into the chocolate mixture and then stir this into the dry ingredients. Mix well.

8. Pour into the prepared pan and bake for 15 – 18 minutes in the hot oven.

9. Do not overcook as brownies should have a chewy center and not be crumbly.

10. Remove the pan from the oven and cool before cutting into 36 x 2 inch (5cm) squares.

Nutritional Facts per brownie: Calories 62, Fat 4.6g, Carbohydrate 4.6g, Dietary Fiber 1.4g, Net Carbs 3.2g, Protein 2.4g.

COCONUT PYRAMIDS

These toasty coconut flavored bites are such an exquisite snack.

Makes 20

INGREDIENTS:

8 large fresh eggs, whites only

2 tsp. vanilla extract

2 tsp. liquid stevia extract (adjust to taste)

3 tbsp. water

4 cups (372g) unsweetened coconut, shredded

DIRECTIONS:

1. Pre-heat the oven to 375°F (191°C).

2. Prepare 2 cookie sheets by covering them with parchment

3. In a large bowl mix the egg whites with a fork to break them down a little.

4. Mix in the vanilla, water and liquid sweetener.

5. Stir in the coconut and mix well.

6. Place heaped tablespoonfuls on the prepared sheets, like little pyramids.

7. Place in the oven and reduce the heat to 325°F (163°C).

8. Make for 12 – 15 minutes until toasty brown on the outside.

9. Remove from the oven and cool completely on a wire rack.

Nutritional Facts per pyramid: Calories 111, Fat 9.7g, Carbohydrate 3.2g, Dietary Fiber 2.1g, Net Carbs 1.1g, Protein 3.4g.

CHOCOLATE CHIP COOKIES

Very chocolaty, chocolate chip cookies – moreish indeed!

Makes 24

INGREDIENTS:

5 ounces (142g) butter, softened

1 large fresh egg

2 tsp. vanilla extract

1 cup (200g) granulated sugar substitute

1¾ cups (168g) almond flour

½ cup (47g) unsweetened coconut, shredded

½ tsp. salt

1 tsp. baking powder

3 ounces (85g) dark chocolate (80% cocoa solids), roughly chopped

DIRECTIONS:

1. Beat the butter until very soft and creamy.

2. Beat in the sugar, eggs and vanilla.

3. In a separate bowl, mix together the almond flour, salt and baking powder. Add half of the coconut.

4. Stir these dry ingredients into the butter mixture making sure everything is well incorporated.

5. Stir in the rest of the coconut and the chocolate pieces.

6. Gather the dough together and place it in plastic wrap.

7. Cool in the fridge for half an hour.

8. Pre-heat the oven to 325°F (163°C).

9. Line 2 cookie trays with parchment.

10. Divide the dough into 24 and place the pieces on the prepared cookie sheets.

11. Press each cookie down with the back of a fork to flatten it.

12. Bake for 25 - 30 minutes, turning the sheets after 18 minutes.

13. Remove from the oven and leave to cool on a wire rack.

14. Store in an airtight container.

Nutritional Facts per cookie: Calories 87, Fat 2.6g, Carbohydrate 3.0g, Dietary Fiber 2.0g, Net Carbs 1.0g, Protein 1.2g.

ALMOND SNAPS

These thin cracker like biscuits are fantastic served with Keto ice-cream!

Makes 40

INGREDIENTS:

1½ cups (144g) almond flour

4 tsp. granulated sugar substitute

2 fresh eggs, white only

¼ tsp. salt

Few drops almond extract

DIRECTIONS:

1. Pre-heat the oven to 325°F (163°C).

2. Mix all of the ingredients together in a medium sized bowl.

3. Divide the dough into 2 halves.

4. Spoon out half of the mixture into a large cookie sheet, no sides, which has been covered with heavy duty foil.

5. Spread the dough out with your fingers, as far as possible, into a large rectangle.

6. Cover the dough with a piece of waxed paper and roll out to as thin as possible to an even shape. Don't worry if the edges are a bit raggedy!

7. Remove the waxed paper and use a sharp knife to cut the dough into squares or triangles.

8. Add the raggedy pieces to the other half of dough.

9. Repeat with the second half of the dough.

10. Bake for 10 - 12 minutes until golden brown.

Nutritional Facts per snap: Calories 9, Fat 0.8g, Carbohydrate 0.3g, Dietary Fiber 0.2g, Net Carbs 0.1g, Protein 0.5g.

SPICY BUTTONS

These little biscuits are made with cinnamon but you can easily change the spice or use a mixture as you fancy.

Makes 24

INGREDIENTS:

¾ cup (72g) almond flour

6 tsp. granulated sugar substitute

1 fresh egg, white only

1 pinch salt

½ tsp. powdered cinnamon or other spice of choice

Few drops vanilla extract

DIRECTIONS:

1. Pre-heat the oven to 325°F (163°C).

2. Prepare 2 cookie sheets with parchment paper.

3. Mix together all of the ingredients in a small bowl.

4. Drop 24 small heaps of dough onto the sheets.

5. Use your fingers to mold into small balls and with a fork press the dough down to make thin biscuits.

6. Do not worry if they are a bit rustic looking as this adds to their charm!

7. Bake in the pre-heated oven for 10 – 12 minutes until brown.

8. Remove from the oven but leave on the sheets to firm for a few minutes before placing on a wire rack to cool completely.

Nutritional Facts per button: Calories 23, Fat 1.9 g, Carbohydrate 0.8g, Dietary Fiber 0.4g, Net Carbs 0.4g, Protein 1.0g.

COOKIES WITH CREAM CHEESE

Serve with a dollop of cream on top or with some sugar free jam.

Makes 24 small cookies

INGREDIENTS:

4 ounce (113g) butter, melted

2 ounces (57g) full fat cream cheese

1 extra-large fresh egg

1 ounce (28g) coconut flour

½ tsp. baking powder

½ tsp. baking soda

¼ tsp. liquid stevia extract (adjust to taste)

½ tsp xanthan gum

½ tsp. vanilla extract

DIRECTIONS:

1. Pre-heat the oven to 350°F (177°C).

2. Line a cookie sheet with parchment paper.

3. Mix together the butter and cream cheese in a bowl making sure that there are no lumps.

4. In a separate bowl mix together the coconut flour, baking powder, xanthan gum and the baking soda.

5. In a separate small bowl add the sugar substitute and vanilla to the egg and beat well together.

6. Add the dry ingredients to the butter and cream cheese and mix well.

7. Stir in the egg mixture and combine everything well together.

8. Drop small spoonfuls of the mixture onto the prepared sheet and bake for 8 – 10 minutes until they are brown around the edges and the centers are cooked.

9. Remove from the oven, cool on the baking sheet for a few minutes before removing to a wire rack to cool completely.

Nutritional Facts per cookie: Calories 51, Fat 5.0g, Carbohydrate 0.9g, Dietary Fiber 0.4g, Net Carbs 0.4g, Protein 0.7g.

PEANUT BUTTER BALLS

No baking with this – quick and easy and just sooooo.... delicious! Careful with these large chocolate coated peanuts, they are moreish. Too many and you'll go over your carb allowance quickly.

Makes 36

INGREDIENTS:

16 ounce (454g) jar smooth peanut butter

1½ cups (192g) peanuts, finely chopped

7 ounces (198g) dark chocolate (70 % cocoa solids)

2 tbsp. light vegetable oil

DIRECTIONS:

1. Chill the peanut butter.

2. Put the chopped peanuts onto a large plate

3. Using a teaspoon, drop spoonfuls of peanut butter onto the chopped peanuts.

4. Roll the peanut butter around to form balls.

5. Place the balls onto a sheet of waxed paper in a suitable container and put in the fridge to harden a little.

6. Meanwhile, break the chocolate into pieces and place in a small ceramic bowl.

7. Melt it over simmering water. Add the oil and stir well.

8. Remove the peanut balls from the fridge and drop them individually into the melted chocolate. Use a teaspoon to remove them and place them back onto clean wax paper.

9. Refrigerate until eaten!

Nutritional Facts per ball: Calories 146, Fat 14.1g, Carbohydrate 5.3g, Dietary Fiber 1.6g, Net Carbs 3.7g, Protein 5.3g.

LEMON AND COCONUT COOKIES

These cookies have a lovely lemon tang amongst the nutty base flavor.

Makes 24

INGREDIENTS:

1 cup (237ml) butter, softened

1 cup (200g) granulated sugar substitute

1½ cups (168g) coconut flour

4 medium fresh eggs

½ tsp. salt

¼ cup (23g) chopped almonds

2 tsp. lemon extract

DIRECTIONS:

1. Pre-heat the oven to 375°F (191°C).

2. Line two cookie sheets with parchment paper.

3. In a medium sized bowl combine the sugar substitute, lemon extract, salt and butter and beat well together.

4. Add the eggs one at a time, beating well after each addition.

5. Stir in the coconut flour.

6. Drop spoonfuls of the biscuit mix onto the prepared sheets, flatten with a fork.

7. Top with a sprinkle of chopped almonds and bake for 12 – 15 minutes in the hot oven.

8. Turn the cookies after 8 minutes to brown evenly.

9. Remove from the oven and cool on a wire rack.

Nutritional Facts per cookie: Calories 118, Fat 9.6g, Carbohydrate 4.7g, Dietary Fiber 2.6g, Net Carbs 2.1g, Protein 2.2g.

CHOCOLATE ORANGE CHUNKS

Really chocolaty with a hint of orange! These biscuits are not too sweet so you could add a few extra drops of liquid sweetener if you prefer.

Makes 16

INGREDIENTS:

3½ ounces (99g) butter, softened

2 cups (192g) almond flour

¾ cup (150g) granulated sugar substitute

2 ounce (57g) dark chocolate (90% cocoa solids), chopped

2 large fresh eggs

1 large orange, zested and juiced (1 tbsp. required of each)

1 tsp. orange extract

¾ tsp. baking powder

½ tsp. baking soda

½ tsp. salt

DIRECTIONS:

1. Pre-heat the oven to 350°F (177°C).

2. Line two cookie sheets with parchment paper.

3. Mix together the butter, orange zest, juice and orange extract.

4. In a separate bowl mix together the flour, baking powder, baking soda, salt and sugar substitute.

5. Add the dry ingredients to the butter mixture and combine well.

6. Stir in the chocolate.

7. Beat the eggs in a separate bowl and fold into the rest of the ingredients.

101 Yummy and Low Carb Ketogenic Savory and Sweet Snacks

8. Spoon the dough onto the prepared cookie sheets – 16 cookies in all.

9. Flatten each cookie with a fork.

10. Bake for 20 – 23 minutes until nicely browned.

11. Remove from the oven and cool on the sheets for a few minutes before transferring the cookies to a wire rack to cool completely.

12. Store in an airtight tin.

Nutritional Facts per chunk: Calories 173, Fat 14.9g, Carbohydrate 5.9g, Dietary Fiber 2.3g, Net Carbs 3.6g, Protein 4.7g.

MINT CHOCOLATE FINGERS

Hmmm… These taste better than an after dinner mint chocolate and are much lower in carbs. Now that is indeed tempting!

Makes 16

INGREDIENTS:

1¾ cups (168g) almond flour

¼ cup (22g) unsweetened cocoa powder

⅓ cup (67g) granulated sugar substitute, plus another 2 tbsp.

½ tsp. baking powder

½ tsp. xanthan gum

¼ tsp. salt

4 ounces (113g) butter, melted

¼ cup (59ml) almond oil

1 large fresh egg, beaten

1½ tsp. peppermint extract

3½ ounces (99g) dark chocolate (90% cocoa solids)

DIRECTIONS:

1. Pre-heat the oven to 375°F (191°C).

2. Line a cookie sheet with parchment paper.

3. Mix together the almond flour, cocoa powder, sweetener, gum, salt and baking powder in a large bowl.

4. In a separate bowl mix together the butter, almond oil, egg and 1 teaspoon peppermint extract.

5. Stir the wet ingredients into the dry ingredients.

6. When the dough starts to come together turn it onto a board to knead a little until smooth.

7. Form into a rectangle about 10 inches by 4 inches (25 x 10cm) and then place on the prepared baking sheet.

8. Bake for 20 – 25 minutes until firm.

9. Remove from the oven and cool.

10. When cool cut into 16 fingers and spread them out on the same baking sheet.

11. Reduce the oven temperature to 250°F and dry the fingers out in the oven for 30 minutes, turning them half way through this time.

12. Leave in the oven, temperature turned off until very crisp and cold.

13. When the fingers are cold melt the chocolate in a basin over simmering water.

14. Add half a teaspoon of peppermint extract and 2 tablespoons of sugar substitute to the melted chocolate. Mix well.

15. Dip the fingers into the melted chocolate and leave until set.

Nutritional Facts per finger: Calories 208, Fat 18.7g, Carbohydrate 5.5g, Dietary Fiber 2.0g, Net Carbs 3.5g, Protein 4.4g.

LEMON MERINGUE SWIRLS

Add chopped nuts to the basic meringue mix or top the swirls with lemon curd. They look so pretty!

Makes 40

INGREDIENTS:

6 large fresh eggs

1 cup (200g) powdered sugar substitute

¼ tsp. cream of tartar

½ tsp. vanilla extract

½ cup (119ml) freshly squeezed lemon juice

3 ounces (85g) butter

DIRECTIONS:

1. Pre-heat the oven to 200°F (93°C).

2. Line 2 cookie sheets with parchment paper.

3. Separate the eggs into 2 separate bowls as follows:

    *   4 egg whites into a large bowl for the meringue

    *   2 whole eggs plus 2 yolks into a smaller bowl for the lemon curd (cover and refrigerate until needed)

4. Beat the 4 egg whites for the meringue with the cream of tartar until soft peaks form.

5. Add ½ a cup (100g) of the powdered sweetener a little at a time and continue beating until stiff peaks form.

6. Gently fold in the vanilla.

7. Spoon the meringue onto the cookie sheets to make 40 small meringues.

8. Using a teaspoon hollow out the center of each one to form 'nests'.

9. Bake in the slow oven for 1 hour and 40 minutes. Turn off the heat and leave the meringues to dry out for a further 3 hours or overnight.

10. When the meringues are crisp make the filling.

11. In a small sauce pan beat together the lemon juice, sweetener and the eggs you have saved in the second bowl.

12. Add the butter and stir continuously over a medium heat until thick.

13. Strain to remove the lemon zest and any lumps that may have formed.

14. Cool the lemon curd.

15. When ready to serve place a teaspoonful of curd in each meringue nest. And enjoy!

Nutritional Facts per swirl: Calories 28, Fat 2.5g, Carbohydrate 0.3g, Dietary Fiber 0g, Net Carbs 0.3g, Protein 1.0g.

CHOCOLATE MERINGUES

Here's a chocolate variation on a meringue treat that you'll be able to enjoy with the entire family.

Makes 48

INGREDIENTS:

8 large fresh eggs, whites only

1 cup (200g) powdered sugar substitute

½ tsp. cream of tartar

4 tbsp. unsweetened cocoa powder

1 tsp. vanilla extract

3½ ounces (99g) dark chocolate

1½ ounces (43g) butter

DIRECTIONS:

1. Pre-heat the oven to 200°F (93°C).

2. Line 2 cookie sheets with parchment paper.

3. Beat the egg whites with the cream of tartar until soft peaks form.

4. Mix the sugar substitute with the cocoa powder.

5. Slowly add the sugar substitute and cocoa mixture, beating well after each addition.

6. Continue beating until stiff peaks form.

7. Fold in the vanilla.

8. Spoon onto the prepared baking sheets.

9. Bake in the slow oven for 1 hour and 40 minutes.

10. Turn off the heat and leave the meringues to dry out for a further 3 hours or overnight.

11. When the meringues are crisp make the chocolate topping.

12. Melt the chocolate over low heat with the butter. Mix well.

13. Drizzle over the meringues. Leave to set.

Nutritional Facts per meringue: Calories 32, Fat 2.4g, Carbohydrate 1.5g, Dietary Fiber 0.4g, Net Carbs 1.1g, Protein 1.3g.

NO BAKE CHOCO CHEWS

These are yummy mouthfuls of bliss to have on hand for that sweet craving.

Makes 24

INGREDIENTS:

4 ounces (113g) butter

3½ ounces (99g) dark chocolate (85% cocoa solids)

2 tbsp. almond butter

½ cup (119ml) coconut cream

1 tsp. almond extract

¼ cup (50g) powdered sugar substitute

2½ cups (233g) unsweetened coconut, flakes

3 cups (279g) unsweetened coconut, shredded

1 ounce (28g) dark chocolate for drizzling

DIRECTIONS:

1. Melt together the chocolate, almond butter and butter in a large saucepan.

2. Add the coconut cream, almond extract and sweetener and stir well together.

3. Add the two types of coconut and stir well to mix everything together.

4. Place spoonfuls onto parchment paper.

5. Melt the extra ounce (28g) of chocolate and drizzle over the chews.

6. Place in the fridge to set and harden. Yum!

Nutritional Facts per chew: Calories 208, Fat 19.3g, Carbohydrate 8.0g, Dietary Fiber 3.1g, Net Carbs 4.9g, Protein 2.2g.

GINGER BITES

Who can resist a ginger biscuit with a cup of tea or coffee? This Keto friendly variation will be sure to hit the spot.

Makes 48

INGREDIENTS:

1½ cups (144g) almond flour

½ tsp. powdered cinnamon

¾ tsp. powdered ginger

¼ tsp. salt

2 large fresh eggs, white only

2½ tbsp. granulated sugar substitute

¼ tsp. vanilla extract

DIRECTIONS:

1. Pre-heat the oven to 325°F (163°C).

2. Line 2 large cookie sheets with parchment paper.

3. In a medium sized bowl mix together the almond flour, cinnamon, ginger and salt.

4. Stir in the sugar substitute and the egg whites, together with the vanilla extract.

5. Place teaspoonfuls onto the prepared cookie sheets and press each one down with the back of a fork to form a flat cookie.

6. Bake in the hot oven for 15 – 20 minutes until golden brown. Turn halfway through the cooking time.

7. Remove from the oven and carefully place the bites on a wire rack to cool.

Nutritional Facts per bite: Calories 16, Fat 1.3g, Carbohydrate 0.8g, Dietary Fiber 0.4g, Net Carbs 0.4g, Protein 0.9g.

NO BAKE NUTTY COOKIES

Here's another wonderful no bake recipe for a busy lifestyle. There's lots of nutty flavors to be enjoyed here!

Makes 32

INGREDIENTS:

2 cups (539g) smooth peanut butter

1 cup (237ml) unsalted butter

1 cup (200g) granulated sugar substitute

2 tsp. almond extract

2 cups (186g) unsweetened coconut, shredded

2¼ cups (245g) pecans, chopped

2¼ cups (263g) walnuts, chopped

½ cup (57g) macadamias, chopped

DIRECTIONS:

1. Line 2 large baking sheets with waxed paper.

2. In a large saucepan over a low heat, warm together the peanut butter and the butter. Stir well to combine.

3. Stir in the sugar substitute, almond extract and the coconut.

4. Stir in the nuts.

5. Drop spoonfuls of the mixture onto the prepared cookie sheets; use your fingers to make nice even shapes.

6. Refrigerate to harden for a few hours.

7. Store in the fridge in an airtight container.

Nutritional Facts per cookie: Calories 287, Fat 27.8g, Carbohydrate 6.5g, Dietary Fiber 2.9g, Net Carbs 3.6g, Protein 7.3g.

MIXED NUT BARS

These mixed nut bars have a hint of chocolate and are great for breakfast and in lunch boxes.

Makes 16

INGREDIENTS:

1¼ cups (160g) mixed nuts of your choice (pecans, almonds, walnuts, macadamias)

¼ cup (57g) butter

¼ cup (23g) toasted unsweetened coconut, shredded

¼ cup (42g) flax seeds

⅓ cup (85g) peanut butter

1 tsp. vanilla extract

½ cup (100g) granulated sugar substitute

2 ounces (57g) dark chocolate, finely chopped

DIRECTIONS:

1. Pre-heat the oven to 375°F (191°C).

2. Prepare a baking tin 12 x 8 inches (30 x 20cm) by lining it with parchment.

3. Chop the nuts together in a processor or blender until chopped roughly.

4. Put them in a large bowl and add the coconut and flax seeds.

5. Melt together the butter and peanut butter. Add the vanilla extract and sugar substitute.

6. Mix this into the nut mixture.

7. Add the chopped chocolate.

8. Spoon into the prepared tin and press down evenly.

9. Bake for 10 – 12 minutes in the hot oven.

10. Remove from the oven and cut into 12 bars, 2 x 3 inches (5 x 7.5cm).

11. Cool on a wire rack and munch away!

Nutritional Facts per bar: Calories 152, Fat 13.0g, Carbohydrate 5.4g, Dietary Fiber 2.4g, Net Carbs 3.0g, Protein 3.9g.

FRUITY FAT BOMBS!

No Keto snack book would be complete without some super delicious fat bombs! Here is the first of three recipes for you to try.

Makes 10

INGREDIENTS:

5 ounces (142g) butter

6 tbsp. coconut oil

4 tbsp. cocoa powder

4 tbsp. sugar free fruit syrup (raspberry is very tasty)

DIRECTIONS:

1. Prepare 10 small molds and place them on a baking sheet – mini heat resistant silicone muffin cases will do.

2. In a small sauce pan combine all of the ingredients over a low heat and stir well.

3. Pour into the molds or use a spoon if you would prefer.

4. Freeze for a few hours.

5. Pop each one out of their mold and enjoy.

6. Keep in the freezer or the bombs will melt!

Nutritional Facts per bomb: Calories 177, Fat 19.9g, Carbohydrate 2.2g, Dietary Fiber 0.7g, Net Carbs 1.5g, Protein 0.5g.

CHOCOLATE COCONUT FAT BOMBS

A stripy fat bomb that is fun to make and even more fun to eat!

Makes 25

INGREDIENTS:

2 cups (474ml) coconut oil

2 tsp. liquid stevia extract (adjust to taste)

4 ounces (113g) unsweetened cocoa

1 cup (227g) salted butter

1½ cups (340g) coconut butter

DIRECTIONS:

1. Prepare 25 small molds and place them on a baking sheet—mini heat resistant silicone muffin cases or other molds will do.

2. Gently melt together the coconut oil, liquid sweetener, cocoa powder and the butter over a low heat.

3. Using a table spoon carefully spoon 1 spoonful of mixture into each mold and freeze for 15 minutes.

4. While the mixture is freezing, melt the coconut butter.

5. Remove the molds from the freezer and spoon a tablespoon of the coconut butter into each one. Refreeze for 15 minutes.

6. Remove from the freezer and top with the rest of the chocolate mix.

7. Place in the freezer and freeze until firm.

8. Store in the freezer!

Nutritional Facts per bomb: Calories 317, Fat 33.8g, Carbohydrate 5.8g, Dietary Fiber 3.2g, Net Carbs 2.6g, Protein 1.8g.

118

LIME FAT BOMBS

These use lime juice and zest, but you could try lemon for a deliciously different flavor.

Makes 10

INGREDIENTS:

1 cup (237ml) coconut oil

¼ cup (57g) butter

1 lime, juiced plus the zest

½ tsp. liquid stevia extract (adjust to taste)

DIRECTIONS:

1. Prepare 10 small molds and place them on a baking sheet – heat resistant mini silicone muffin cases will do.

2. Combine the coconut oil and butter in a small saucepan and heat over a gentle heat until they become liquid.

3. Remove from heat, add the zest and lime, and blend for a few minutes until smooth. The aim is for the lime to start to set into the cooling mixture otherwise it will separate in the freezer.

4. Carefully pour into the prepared molds.

5. Freeze until required.

6. Store in the freezer!

Nutritional Facts per bomb: Calories 233, Fat 26.4g, Carbohydrate 1.4g, Dietary Fiber 0.4g, Net Carbs 1.0g, Protein 1.4g.

TIRAMISU TREATS

Be daring and try out these little icy tiramisu flavored pops.

Makes 8

INGREDIENTS:

4 ounces (113g) coconut cream

4 ounces (113g) cream cheese

1½ cups (356ml) coconut milk

8 tbsp. powdered sugar substitute

2 tbsp. instant coffee powder

8 tbsp. coconut oil

2 ounces (57g) unsweetened cocoa powder

½ tsp. liquid stevia extract (adjust to taste)

1 tsp. rum extract

DIRECTIONS:

1. Mix together the coconut cream, cream cheese, coconut milk, powdered sugar substitute. Half the rum extract and the coffee powder.

2. Pour into ice cube trays and freeze until hard – about 2 hours.

3. Meanwhile warm the coconut oil and add the cocoa, liquid sweetener and the rest of the rum extract. Cool.

4. When the 'ice cubes' have frozen pop them out of the trays and dip them in the chocolate mixture.

5. Place individually on parchment paper and re-freeze until required.

Nutritional Facts per treat: Calories 323, Fat 33.6g, Carbohydrate 8.2g, Dietary Fiber 3.7g, Net Carbs 4.5g, Protein 3.8g.

COCONUT LEMON BALLS

Chilly little mouthfuls of fresh citrus will get your taste buds tingling!

Makes 20

INGREDIENTS:

16 ounces (454g) full fat cream cheese

2 cups (186g) unsweetened coconut, shredded

2 limes, juiced and zested

1 lemon, juiced and zested

⅓ cup (67g) powdered sugar substitute (adjust to taste)

DIRECTIONS:

1. Beat the cream cheese very well with the juice and zest of the lime and lemon. A processor will help here!

2. Beat in half of the coconut and the sweetener.

3. Form into 20 little balls and place on waxed paper. Refrigerate overnight.

4. The next day roll the balls in the rest of the coconut.

5. Store in the fridge until ready to eat.

Nutritional Facts per ball: Calories 124, Fat 11.8g, Carbohydrate 3.3g, Dietary Fiber 1.3g, Net Carbs 2.0g, Protein 2.2g.

CHOCO ALMOND TRUFFLES

Mmmm... Little morsels of creamy, buttery, choc-nut explosions that you'll simply love.

Makes 24

INGREDIENTS:

8 ounces (227g) dark chocolate (80% cocoa solids)

4 tbsp. butter

4 tbsp. heavy cream

1 tsp. almond extract

¼ tsp. vanilla extract

¼ tsp. liquid stevia extract (adjust to taste)

DIRECTIONS:

1. Prepare 24 mini muffin cups and place on a baking sheet.

2. Melt the chocolate and the butter in a ceramic bowl over simmering water.

3. Cool before stirring in the cream, almond vanilla essence, and sweetener.

4. Spoon into the cups and freeze until firm.

5. Store in the freezer or the refrigerator.

Nutritional Facts per truffle: Calories 82, Fat 7.4g, Carbohydrate 3.7g, Dietary Fiber 1.3g, Net Carbs 2.4g, Protein 0.8g.

CREAMY CHOCOLATE FUDGE

Pop in the mouth squares of buttery chocolate fudge, are yours to command!

Makes 16 squares

INGREDIENTS:

4 tbsp. butter

1 cup (237ml) heavy cream

8 ounces (227g) plain, full fat cream cheese

6 drops liquid stevia extract (adjust to taste)

4 tbsp. unsweetened cocoa powder

¼ tsp. salt

DIRECTIONS:

1. Line a small baking tin with foil.

2. Melt the butter in a saucepan over a low heat.

3. Remove from the heat and add the cream and cream cheese.

4. Whisk until smooth. Add the sugar substitute.

5. Replace on the heat and heat carefully until beginning to bubble, stir constantly.

6. Remove from the heat again and beat in the cocoa and the salt.

7. Pour the fudge into the prepared tin and cool.

8. Place in the refrigerator until set – about 4 hours.

9. Turn out of the tin, cut into 16 squares. Keep in the fridge.

Nutritional Facts per square: Calories 104, Fat 10.8g, Carbohydrate 1.3g, Dietary Fiber 0.4g, Net Carbs 0.9g, Protein 1.5g.

BUTTERSCOTCH NUT SQUARES

These are basically a fat bomb mixture with the added crunch of pecans. Try using other nuts if you have them, and substitute caramel extract for the butterscotch if you are feeling adventurous!

Make 16 squares

INGREDIENTS:

2 cups (454g) coconut butter

4 ounces (113g) salted butter

1 tsp. butterscotch extract

½ cup (55g) pecan pieces, roasted

10 drops liquid stevia extract (adjust to taste)

DIRECTIONS:

1. Line a small baking tin with foil.

2. In a small saucepan over a low heat, soften the coconut butter and butter.

3. Remove from the heat and stir in the sweetener, flavoring and toasted nuts.

4. Pour into the prepared tin and cool.

5. Place in the refrigerator until set – about 4 hours.

6. Turn out of the tin, cut into 16 squares. Keep in the fridge.

Nutritional Facts per square: Calories 263, Fat 26.4g, Carbohydrate 7.5g, Dietary Fiber 5.4g, Net Carbs 2.1g, Protein 2.5g.

CHOCOLATE AND COCONUT CUPCAKES

Cupcakes are the all-time favorite of children worldwide – try this Keto version for any time or perhaps a birthday cupcake to send to school on that special day!

Makes 12

INGREDIENTS:

5 large fresh eggs

½ cup (119ml) coconut oil

1 cup (237ml) coconut cream

1 tsp. vanilla extract

¾ cup (150g) powdered sugar substitute

½ cup (56g) coconut flour

1 tsp. baking powder

½ tsp. salt

4 ounces (113g) butter

4 ounces (113g) cream cheese

4 tbsp. unsweetened cocoa powder

½ cup (118ml) heavy cream

2 ounces (57g) dark chocolate (75% cocoa solids)

12 pecan nut halves to garnish or grated chocolate

DIRECTIONS:

1. Pre-heat the oven to 350°F (177°C).

2. Prepare a 12 cup muffin pan by lining with paper cases.

3. In a large bowl, beat the eggs together well.

4. Add the coconut cream, vanilla and ¼ cup (50g) of powdered sugar substitute.

5. In a separate bowl mix together the coconut flour, baking powder and salt.

6. Stir these dry ingredients into the egg mixture and mix well.

7. Spoon into the prepared muffin cups and bake for 20 – 23 minutes until cooked.

8. Leave to cool in the muffin pan for 5 minutes before removing to a wire rack to cool completely.

9. When the cakes are cool make the icing by first melting the chocolate over a low heat. Leave to cool.

10. Beat together the butter, cream cheese, the rest of the powdered sweetener and the cocoa powder.

11. Beat in the cooled melted chocolate.

12. Whip the cream in a separate bowl and fold into the rest of the icing ingredients.

13. Put the icing into a piping bag and pipe swirls onto of the cooled cupcakes.

14. Decorate with a pecan half or some grated chocolate.

Nutritional Facts per cupcake: Calories 427, Fat 41.0g, Carbohydrate 10.5g, Dietary Fiber 3.3g, Net Carbs 7.2g, Protein 6.5g.

CARAMEL SQUARES

These yummy sweet squares contain both caramel and chocolate for good measure!

Makes 24

INGREDIENTS:

1 cup (237ml) water

1¾ cups (350g) granulated sugar substitute

½ cup (118ml) heavy cream

8 ounces (227g) butter

1 tsp. salt

½ tsp. xanthan gum

2¾ cups (264g) almond flour

½ tsp. vanilla extract

3½ ounces (99g) dark chocolate (85% cocoa solids), grated

DIRECTIONS:

1. Make the caramel first as it needs to cool.

2. In a heavy based saucepan dissolve 1 cup (200g) sugar substitute with the water. Stir until just dissolved.

3. Bring to the boil over a medium heat and boil, without stirring, for 7 minutes.

4. The mixture should have darkened in color, if not, boil for a few seconds longer. Do not let it get too dark.

5. Remove from the heat and stir in the cream, 1 ounce (28g) butter and ½ teaspoon salt. Be careful as it will bubble and spit!

6. Sprinkle in the gum and stir well to remove any lumps. Set aside.

7. Pre-heat the oven to 325°F (163°C).

8. Prepare a 13 x 9 inch (33 x 23cm) pan by lining it with parchment.

9. In a bowl, combine the almond flour, ½ teaspoon salt and ¾ cup (150g) sugar substitute.

10. Rub in 7 ounces (198g) butter until the mixture looks like bread crumbs. (Use a processor if you have one!). Stir in the vanilla.

11. Add the chocolate and mix through.

12. Press half of the mixture into the prepared tin and bake in the hot oven for 8 minutes.

13. Remove the tin from the oven and spoon over the previously prepared caramel.

14. Top with the rest of the crumb mixture and return to the oven to bake for a further 10 – 12 minutes.

15. Remove from the oven and leave to cool completely before cutting into bars.

Nutritional Facts per square: Calories 123, Fat 12.3g, Carbohydrate 2.8g, Dietary Fiber 0.9g, Net Carbs 1.9g, Protein 1.2g.

CHEESECAKE BITES

These mini cheesecakes with a spicy base, will slide over your tongue in a sweet cascade of happiness!

Makes 24

INGREDIENTS:

2 cups (192g) almond flour

½ cup (100g) granulated sugar substitute

2 tsp. mixed spice

½ tsp. baking soda

½ tsp. salt

½ tsp. xanthan gum

1 large fresh egg, beaten

⅓ cup (79ml) coconut butter, warmed

1 tbsp. molasses

6 ounces (170g) full fat cream cheese

4 tbsp. powdered sugar substitute

½ tsp. vanilla extract

DIRECTIONS:

1. Pre-heat the oven to 350°F (177°C).

2. Prepare 24 mini muffin cups with paper cases.

3. In a large bowl mix together the almond flour, granulated sugar substitute, mixed spice, baking soda, salt and gum.

4. Stir in the egg, coconut butter and molasses until the dough starts to come together.

5. Divide the dough into 24 small even sixed pieces and press each one into the bottom of a mini muffin cup.

6. Use your index finger to make a well in the center of each piece of dough and gently push some of the dough up the sides of each cup.

7. Beat together the cream cheese, powdered sugar substitute and vanilla.

8. Using a teaspoon, spoon this mixture evenly among the mini muffin cups.

9. Place into the hot oven and bake for 10 – 12 minutes until lightly brown and the filling is set.

10. Remove from the oven and cool.

Nutritional Facts per bite: Calories 73, Fat 5.9g, Carbohydrate 3.8g, Dietary Fiber 0.7g, Net Carbs 3.1g, Protein 1.6g.

CHOCOLATE CHEESECAKE

A delicious cheesecake to cut and serve in slices rather than individual mini bites.

Serves 8

INGREDIENTS:

1¼ cups (120g) almond meal

4 tbsp. unsweetened cocoa powder

3 tbsp. butter, melted

12 ounces (340g) cream cheese

2 large fresh eggs

1 tsp. vanilla extract

1 cup (200g) powdered sugar substitute

DIRECTIONS:

1. Pre-heat the oven to 350°F (177°C).

2. Butter a deep round 8 inch (20cm) oven proof dish.

3. Mix together the almond meal, 2 tbsp. cocoa and the melted butter in a small bowl.

4. Press this mixture firmly into the base of the prepared dish.

5. Bake for 12 – 15 minutes.

6. Meanwhile prepare the cheese filling by beating together the cream cheese, egg, vanilla, the rest of the cocoa and the sweetener.

7. Remove the base from the oven and pour over the cheese mixture.

8. Replace in the hot oven and bake for about 75 minutes until firm on the outside but still a little wobbly in the middle.

9. Remove from the oven and cool completely. Put in the fridge for a couple of hours before slicing and serving.

Nutritional Facts per slice: Calories 330, Fat 30.1g, Carbohydrate 7.1g, Dietary Fiber 2.8g, Net Carbs 4.3g, Protein 9.7g.

ALMOND CHEESY CUPCAKES

Here's a cheesecake favorite in yet another guise, cupcakes! These have a lovely almond flavor!

Makes 12

INGREDIENTS:

2 ounces (57g) butter, melted

½ cup (48g) almond meal

16 ounces (454g) cream cheese

¾ cup (150g) granulated sugar substitute

2 large fresh eggs

1 tsp. almond extract

DIRECTIONS:

1. Pre-heat the oven to 350°F (177°C).

2. Prepare 12 muffin cups with paper cases.

3. Stir the almond meal into the melted butter.

4. Spoon this mixture evenly among the prepared cupcake cases and press it down with the back of a spoon.

5. Beat together the cream cheese, eggs, sugar substitute and the almond extract until smooth.

6. Divide among the cupcake cases, filling them almost to the top.

7. Bake in the hot oven for 15 – 18 minutes.

8. Remove from the oven and cool completely before serving.

9. Chill in the fridge once cold, and then serve.

Nutritional Facts per cupcake: Calories 211, Fat 20.3g, Carbohydrate 2.5g, Dietary Fiber 0.5g, Net Carbs 2.0g, Protein 5.1g.

COCONUT PIKELETS

Pancakes, scotch pancakes, flapjacks? Whatever you call them; these are delicious as a standby recipe for a snack, dessert or even breakfast!

Makes 6

INGREDIENTS:

½ cup (56g) coconut flour

3 tbsp. granulated sugar substitute

6 large fresh eggs

½ tsp. baking powder

½ tsp. salt

2 ounces (57g) butter, melted

1 cup (237ml) coconut milk

1 tsp. vanilla extract

DIRECTIONS:

1. Pre-heat a griddle to medium low.

2. Beat the eggs in a large bowl until light and fluffy and then beat in the coconut milk, vanilla and sugar substitute.

3. Add the coconut flour, baking powder and salt and beat well.

4. Stir in the melted butter.

5. Grease the griddle with a little butter and pour 2 large tablespoons of mixture onto it. Spread it out to a circle of about 3 inches (7.5cm) in diameter.

6. If your griddle is large enough put on another one or two lots of mixture.

7. Griddle for about 3 minutes on one side until the top is set around the edges.

8. Carefully flip over and brown on the other side.

9. Serve warm with lots of farm fresh butter! And perhaps, some sugar free jam?

Nutritional Facts per pikelet: Calories 276, Fat 23.2g, Carbohydrate 8.6g, Dietary Fiber 4.2g, Net Carbs 4.4g, Protein 8.6g.

GINGER MUFFINS

Muffins are always a firm favorite and these have a really exotic ginger taste you'll relish.

Makes 12

INGREDIENTS:

6 large fresh eggs, beaten

1 cup (96g) almond flour

3 tbsp. coconut flour

5 tbsp. grape seed oil

2½ ounces (71g) butter

1 tbsp. powdered ginger

1 tsp. baking powder

1 cup (200g) granulated sugar substitute

½ tsp. salt

DIRECTIONS:

1.   Pre-heat the oven to 350°F (177°C).

2.   Prepare 12 muffin cups with paper cases.

3.   Combine all of the dry ingredients in a medium bowl – mix well.

4.   Add the egg, oil and butter to the dry ingredients and mix until smooth.

5.   Divide among the prepared muffin cups and bake in the hot oven for 20 – 23 minutes.

6.   When cooked remove from the oven and cool a little on a wire rack. Serve warm.

Nutritional Facts per muffin: Calories 201, Fat 18.3g, Carbohydrate 4.2g, Dietary Fiber 1.7g, Net Carbs 2.5g, Protein 5.8g.

ORANGE CHEESE CAKE

A tangy cheese cake without a crust? More like a baked cheese custard – smooth and utterly scrumptious!

Makes 8

INGREDIENTS:

1 cup (237ml) heavy cream

8 ounces (227g) cream cheese

2 large fresh eggs, beaten

1½ tsp. liquid stevia extract (adjust to taste)

1 large orange zested and juiced (4 tbsp. juice)

DIRECTIONS:

1. Pre-heat the oven to 350°F (177°C).

2. Grease 8 x 6 ounce (170g) individual oven proof dishes with butter.

3. Beat together the cream cheese and the heavy cream until smooth.

4. Whisk in the liquid sweetener, orange juice and zest.

5. Beat in the eggs until just combined.

6. Divide the mixture evenly among the prepared dishes.

7. Place the dishes on a baking sheet and bake for 30 – 35 minutes until just set.

8. Turn off the oven and leave the dishes to stand for 5 minutes before removing them from the oven and allowing to cool completely.

9. When cool refrigerate for a couple of hours to chill before serving.

Nutritional Facts per portion: Calories 179, Fat 16.7g, Carbohydrate 4.0g, Dietary Fiber 0.6g, Net Carbs 3.4g, Protein 4.2g.

ICED CINNAMON ROLLS

These come out just like a rolled cinnamon bun with cream cheese icing and the delicious spicy smell of these cooking instantly shouts, 'More!'

Makes 16

INGREDIENTS:

4 cups (384g) almond flour

4 tbsp. granulated sugar substitute

4 tsp. baking powder

1 tsp. baking soda

1 tsp. salt

3½ tsp. powdered cinnamon

2 large fresh eggs, beaten

4 ½ ounces (128g) butter, melted

6 tbsp. heavy cream

1½ tsp. vanilla extract

1 tsp. liquid stevia extract (adjust to taste)

2 ounces (57g) cream cheese

DIRECTIONS:

1. Pre-heat the oven to 325°F (163°C).

2. Line 2 baking sheets with parchment.

3. In a medium bowl mix together the almond flour, granulated sugar substitute, baking powder, baking soda, salt and 1 tsp cinnamon.

4. Mix together the egg, 3½ ounces (99g) melted butter, 4 tablespoons cream, 1 tsp vanilla and ½ tsp liquid sugar substitute.

5. Stir the egg mixture into the dry ingredients until a dough forms.

6. On a piece of waxed paper roll or pat out the dough to form a rectangle about 8 x 12 inches (20 x 30cm).

7. Sprinkle on the remaining cinnamon powder.

8. Roll the dough up from the short end – not too tightly as the dough will expand as it cooks.

9. Using a sharp knife cut the roll into 16 x half inch (1.25cm) slices and place them cut side down on the prepared baking sheets.

10. Bake in the hot oven for about 20 minutes until the rolls are firm and a light brown.

11. Remove from the oven and leave the rolls to cool on a wire rack before icing.

12. For the icing beat together the cream cheese, the remaining butter, vanilla and liquid sweetener.

13. Spread the icing over the cooled buns and serve.

Nutritional Facts per roll: Calories 281, Fat 25.4g, Carbohydrate 6.1g, Dietary Fiber 3.0 g, Net Carbs 3.1g, Protein 8.2g.

CHOCOLATE NUT ICE CREAM

Chocolate and peanut heaven in an ice cream – yummo!

Serves 6

INGREDIENTS:

2 cups (452g) smooth cottage cheese

1 cup (232g) cream cheese

3 ounces (85g) chocolate protein powder

6 tbsp. smooth peanut butter

6 tbsp. heavy cream

¾ tsp. liquid stevia extract (adjust to taste)

DIRECTIONS:

1. Place all of the ingredients in a food processor or blender and mix until everything is smooth and creamy.

2. Churn in an ice cream maker if you have one or place in a freezer proof container and place in the freezer.

3. If you are not churning the ice cream stir every 30 minutes as it is freezing to break up any ice crystals.

4. Freeze until required.

5. When ready to serve remove from the freezer about 10 minutes before serving to defrost a little.

Nutritional Facts per portion: Calories 404, Fat 29.3g, Carbohydrate 9.3g, Dietary Fiber 1.3g, Net Carbs 8.0g, Protein 27.7g.

STRAWBERRY ICE CREAM

Warning, you may want to portion this ice cream out, as it is so delicious that you may be tempted to eat it all in one sitting...

Serves 8

INGREDIENTS:

1½ cups (355ml) heavy cream

1 cup (232g) full fat cream cheese

1¼ cups (180g) fresh strawberries

1 tsp. vanilla extract

1 tbsp. xanthan gum

½ lemon, juiced

1 tbsp. powdered sugar substitute

½ tsp. liquid stevia extract (adjust to taste)

DIRECTIONS:

1. Mash the strawberries.

2. Place all of the other ingredients in a large bowl and beat well together.

3. Stir in the strawberries.

4. Churn in an ice cream maker if you have one or place in a freezer proof container and place in the freezer.

5. If you are not churning the ice cream stir every 30 minutes as it is freezing to break up any ice crystals.

6. Freeze until required.

7. When ready to serve remove from the freezer about 10 minutes before serving to defrost a little.

Nutritional Facts per portion: Calories 189, Fat 18.5g, Carbohydrate 4.4g, Dietary Fiber 1.4g, Net Carbs 3.0g, Protein 2.9g.

CHOCOLATE CHIP COCONUT ICE CREAM

This tropical ice cream is made with coconut milk and coconut cream rather than cream and cream cheese. You'll discover lovely chunks of chocolate and toasted coconut that give it a satisfying texture.

Serves 6

INGREDIENTS:

6 ounce (170g) can coconut milk

6 ounce (170g) can coconut cream

½ cup (100g) powdered sugar substitute

½ tsp. xanthan gum

1 tsp. vanilla extract

2 ounces (57g) dark chocolate, chopped

½ cup (47g) unsweetened shredded coconut, toasted

DIRECTIONS:

1. Whisk together the coconut milk, cream, sugar substitute and the gum.

2. Stir in the vanilla extract.

3. Churn in an ice cream maker if you have one or place in a freezer proof container and place in the freezer.

4. If you are not churning the ice cream stir every 30 minutes as it is freezing to break up any ice crystals.

5. Once half frozen stir in the chopped chocolate and the coconut.

6. Freeze until required.

7. When ready to serve remove from the freezer about 10 minutes before serving to defrost a little.

Nutritional Facts per portion: Calories 379, Fat 27.8g, Carbohydrate 14.7g, Dietary Fiber 2.5g, Net Carbs 12.2g, Protein 4.5g.

CHOCOLATE CHIP PECAN BARS

An interesting creation can be enjoyed with this layered bar with a wonderful combination of pecans and chocolate!

Makes 16

INGREDIENTS:

1 cup (96g) almond flour

¾ cup (83g) pecans, very finely chopped

3 large fresh eggs

1 cup (200g) granulated sugar substitute

2 ounces (57g) butter, softened

¼ tsp. xanthan gum

½ tsp. cinnamon

Pinch salt

16 ounces (454g) cream cheese

½ cup (85g) dark chocolate chips

2 tsp. vanilla extract

DIRECTIONS:

1. Pre-heat the oven to 350°F (177°C).

2. Grease a 9 inch (23cm) square pan with a little butter.

3. Mix together the almond flour, butter, ½ cup (100g) sugar substitute, half the vanilla, 1 egg, xanthan gum, cinnamon, pecans and the salt.

4. Press the dough into the base of the prepared pan.

5. Beat together the rest of the ingredients except the chocolate chips.

6. Stir in the chocolate chips.

7. Pour this over the dough base and bake for 30 minutes until the topping is set.

8. Remove from the oven and cool.

9. Cut into bars and serve.

Nutritional Facts per bar: Calories 247, Fat 22.7g, Carbohydrate 6.2g, Dietary Fiber 1.4g, Net Carbs 4.8g, Protein 6.0g.

ALMOND CAKE

This delicious plain cake with a hint of almond has a really low carb count per slice. Superb!

Serves 12

INGREDIENTS:

4 ounces (113g) butter

½ cup (116g) full fat cream cheese

1 cup (200g) granulated sugar substitute

5 large fresh eggs

2 cups (192g) almond flour

1 tsp. baking powder

1 tsp. lemon essence

1 tsp. almond essence

DIRECTIONS:

1. Pre-heat the oven to 350°F (177°C).

2. Line a 9 inch (23cm) round cake pan with parchment.

3. Cream together in a bowl the butter, cream cheese and sugar substitute.

4. Beat in the eggs one at a time.

5. In a separate bowl, mix together the baking powder and the almond flour.

6. Add the flour mixture to the egg mixture a little at a time beating well between additions.

7. Stir in the lemon and almond extracts.

8. Pour into the prepared cake tin and bake for 45 – 50 minutes until cooked.

9. Remove from the oven, turn out onto a wire rack and cool

completely before cutting and serving.

Nutritional Facts per slice: Calories 258, Fat 23.1g, Carbohydrate 5.2g, Dietary Fiber 2.0g, Net Carbs 3.2g, Protein 8.1g.

PECAN PIE

A superb pie to serve at any time of the year to your family and friends. Remember to keep a piece for yourself!

Serves 8

INGREDIENTS:

1½ cups (144g) plus 1 tbsp. almond flour

1½ cups (300g) plus 3 tbsp. granulated sugar substitute

¼ tsp. baking soda

2 ounces (57g) butter

1 tbsp. molasses

2 large fresh eggs

½ cup (119ml) coconut oil

2 tbsp. coconut cream

1 tsp. vanilla extract

2 cups (218g) pecan nuts, halved and chopped in equal portions

---

DIRECTIONS:

1. Pre-heat the oven to 350°F (177°C).

2. Grease a 9 inch (23cm) round pie dish.

3. Combine 1½ cups (144g) almond flour, 1½ cups (300g) sugar substitute, baking soda and the butter in a bowl.

4. Spoon into the base of the prepared pie dish.

5. Using your fingers ensure that the mixture goes up the side of the pie dish and press down carefully to form the pie crust.

6. Bake for 7 minutes until golden brown.

7. Remove the crust from the oven and cool.

8. Reduce the oven heat to 325°F (163°C).

9. Beat together the rest of the ingredients except the pecan nuts.

10. Sprinkle the chopped nuts into the pie shell and top with the egg mixture.

11. Arrange the half pecans on top.

12. Bake uncovered for 30- 35 minutes. Cover with a piece of foil and continue cooking for a further 25 minutes.

13. Remove the pie from the oven and serve warm with whipped cream.

Nutritional Facts per portion: Calories 591, Fat 57.3g, Carbohydrate 13.6g, Dietary Fiber 6.1g, Net Carbs 7.5g, Protein 11.2g.

CARROT LOAF

This tasty carrot loaf topped with cream cheese icing and a suitably low carbohydrate count per slice will be popular for a mid-afternoon snack.

Makes 16 slices

INGREDIENTS:

3½ ounces (99g) almond flour

2 tsp. baking powder

1 tsp. baking soda

4 tbsp. coconut oil, warmed

3½ ounces (99g) grated carrot

1 large fresh egg

1½ tsp. mixed spice

2 tbsp. orange zest

⅓ cup (67g) granulated sugar substitute

3½ ounces (99g) cream cheese

4 drops liquid stevia extract (adjust to taste)

2 tsp. vanilla extract

1 tbsp. heavy cream

DIRECTIONS:

1. Pre-heat the oven to 350°F (177°C).

2. Grease a loaf tin and line with parchment paper.

3. Mix the coconut oil, granulated sugar substitute, and eggs and beat well together.

4. In a separate bowl mix together the flour, baking powder, baking soda and mixed spice. Add to the egg mixture.

5. Stir in the carrot and orange zest.

6. Spoon into the prepared loaf tin and bake in the hot oven for 20 – 25 minutes.

7. Remove from the oven and cool on a wire rack.

8. Make the topping by beating together the cream cheese, liquid sugar substitute, vanilla and heavy cream.

9. Spread over the top of the cooled loaf.

Nutritional Facts per portion: Calories 101, Fat 9.3g, Carbohydrate 2.4g, Dietary Fiber 0.9g, Net Carbs 1.5g, Protein 2.4g.

LITTLE HEAVENLY CLOUDS

Little fluffy morsels of scrumptiousness, what more can I say!

Makes 16

INGREDIENTS:

7 ounces (198g) full fat cream cheese

7 ounces (198g) butter

1 tsp. liquid stevia extract (adjust to taste)

2½ tsp. unsweetened cocoa powder

DIRECTIONS:

1. Beat together all of the ingredients very well until you have a creamy consistency.

2. Spoon into 16 mini muffin cases and place in the freezer until hard.

3. Serve and enjoy!

Nutritional Facts per cloud: Calories 133, Fat 14.4g, Carbohydrate 0.5g, Dietary Fiber 0.1g, Net Carbs 0.4g, Protein 1.1g.

CHOCOLATE CAKE

These little square classic cakes provide a delicious morsel of heaven.

Makes 16 squares

INGREDIENTS:

½ cup (114g) butter

7 ounces (198g) dark chocolate (80% cocoa solids)

4 fresh eggs

1 cup (237ml) heavy fresh cream

1 tsp. liquid stevia extract (adjust to taste)

1 tsp. vanilla extract

2 tsp. baking soda

DIRECTIONS:

1. Pre-heat the oven to 350°F (177°C).

2. Line an 8 x 8 inch (20 x 20cm) square baking pan with foil or parchment.

3. In a small saucepan melt the butter and chocolate and allow it to cool.

4. Beat the eggs together and add in the rest of the ingredients, beating until well mixed.

5. Pour into the prepared baking pan and bake for 30 – 35 minutes until firm.

6. Remove from the oven and cool on a cake rack.

7. Cut into 16 squares.

8. Serve with whipped fresh cream if liked and a sprinkling of grated chocolate

Nutritional Facts per square: Calories 167, Fat 15.7g, Carbohydrate 5.0g, Dietary Fiber 1.7g, Net Carbs 3.3g, Protein 2.6g.

ALMOND COCO BUTTER BARS

A great, tray bake to keep as a standby for that 'cookie craving moment'.

Makes 12

INGREDIENTS:

½ cup (119ml) coconut butter, melted

1¼ cups (120g) almond flour

1 cup (200g) granulated sugar substitute

1 large fresh egg

½ tsp. baking powder

DIRECTIONS:

1. Pre-heat the oven to 350°F (177°C).

2. Line an 8 x 8 inch (20 x 20cm) baking tin with parchment. Line a baking sheet with parchment.

3. Beat together all of the ingredients in a large bowl until well combined.

4. Spoon into the prepared baking tin and bake for 18 – 20 minutes until golden brown.

5. Remove from the oven and cut into 12 bars.

6. Remove from the tin and place apart on the baking sheet.

7. Return to the oven and cook for a further 5 – 8 minutes.

8. Remove from the oven and cool completely before serving.

Nutritional Facts per bar: Calories 88, Fat 7.7g, Carbohydrate 3.8g, Dietary Fiber 2.0g, Net Carbs 1.8g, Protein 1.7g.

CREAM CUSTARDS

Enjoy these creamy little puddings with a coffee flavor!

Makes 8

INGREDIENTS:

4 cups (946ml) heavy cream

4 tsp. instant coffee

8 large fresh eggs, yolks only

2 cups (400g) granulated sugar substitute

½ tsp. salt

3 tsp. vanilla extract

DIRECTIONS:

1. Pre-heat the oven into 350°F (177°C).

2. Butter 8 ramekin or custard cups and place in a roasting tin with cold water around them to come up to half the depth of the ramekins.

3. Gently heat together the cream and the coffee – do not boil.

4. Whisk together the rest of the ingredients and then gradually whisk in the hot coffee cream.

5. Divide equally among the prepared ramekins.

6. Bake in the hot oven for 30 – 40 minutes until set.

7. Remove from the oven, cool and leave to chill in the fridge for a couple of hours before serving.

Nutritional Facts per portion: Calories 275, Fat 26.7g, Carbohydrate 5.0g, Dietary Fiber 0g, Net Carbs 5.0g, Protein 3.9g.

POPPY SEED CAKE

Here's a great basic cake. Bake round or as a slab – whatever you fancy!

Serves 12

INGREDIENTS:

3 ounces (85g) coconut flour

10 ounces (284g) full fat thick plain yogurt

1 lemon, juiced and zested

2 tbsp. poppy seeds

1 tsp. liquid stevia extract (adjust to taste)

2 tsp. baking powder

4 ounces (113g) butter, melted

7 large fresh eggs

DIRECTIONS:

1. Pre-heat the oven into 375°F (191°C).

2. Prepare a baking tin of your choice – about 8 x 11 inches (20 x 28cm) – by lining it with parchment.

3. Beat together the yogurt, sweetener and eggs.

4. Beat in the melted butter.

5. Mix together the coconut flour and the baking powder and stir it into the egg mixture.

6. Add the lemon zest and juice as well as the poppy seeds.

7. Mix until well combined. Pour into the prepared baking tin and bake for 25 – 30 minutes until cooked.

8. Remove from oven and cool on a rack. Cut into 12 and serve.

Nutritional Facts per portion: Calories 173, Fat 13.1g, Carbohydrate 6.3g, Dietary Fiber 2.8g, Net Carbs 3.5g, Protein 7.2g.

SUMMERTIME POPSICLE

This is not just for the children – make enough for the whole family! Use an ice-lolly mold if you have or otherwise freeze in small narrow mugs and insert an ice-cream stick into each.

Makes 6

INGREDIENTS:

1 cup (237ml) coconut cream

1 cup (237ml) unsweetened almond milk

3 tbsp. unsweetened cocoa powder

1 tsp. vanilla extract

¼ tsp. liquid stevia extract (adjust to taste)

DIRECTIONS:

1. Place all of the ingredients except the sweetener in jug and blend until smooth.

2. Pour into 4 molds and place in the freezer. (Remember to put the sticks in!)

3. Freeze for several hours.

4. Enjoy!

Nutritional Facts per portion: Calories 136, Fat 13.5, Carbohydrate 4.7g, Dietary Fiber 2.2g, Net Carbs 2.5g, Protein 1.9g.

HOT CHOCOLATE NIGHTCAP

A hot chocolate nightcap recipe to complete the recipe book!

Serves 4

INGREDIENTS:

2 cups (474ml) unsweetened almond milk

2 cups (473ml) heavy cream

2 ounces (57g) unsweetened cocoa powder

Powdered sugar substitute or liquid stevia extract (adjust to taste)

DIRECTIONS:

1. Place all of the ingredients except the sweetener in a large saucepan and heat together over a medium heat.

2. Stir well to mix thoroughly and bring to just under boiling point.

3. Pour into 4 mugs and sweeten to taste.

4. Yummmmmmm!

Nutritional Facts per portion: Calories 254, Fat 25.4g, Carbohydrate 9.9g, Dietary Fiber 5.2g, Net Carbs 4.7g, Protein 4.5g.

THANK YOU

If you enjoyed these recipes, and I'm guessing your taste buds did, please look for other titles in the Keto Living range.

You may enjoy my all course recipe books;

Keto Living Cookbook: Lose Weight with 101 Delicious & Low Carb Ketogenic Recipes

For another, replete with beautiful photography look for;

Keto Living 3 - Color Cookbook: Lose Weight with 101 All New Delicious & Low Carb Ketogenic Recipes

And now available, a guide to the unique protocol of Fat Fasting;

Keto Living – Fat Fast Cookbook: A Guide to Fasting for Weight Loss Including 50 Low Carb & High Fat Recipes

Thanks so much to my family, my friends and the Keto community for keeping me loving all things Keto and making me smile every day.

Be good to each other!

Ella Coleman

35188105R00101

Made in the USA
Lexington, KY
01 September 2014